JOE,

LIKE WORDS PRINTED IN A BOOK,
MEMORIES OF SOMEONE WE'VE
LOST WILL LAST A LIFETIME. I
HOPE THE WORDS ON PAGES 35
AND 62 STIR UP SOME HAPPY
MEMORIES OF SOMEONE CLOSE TO
YOU.

JEFF

Hunting Camp ALMANAC

A Compendium of Stories, Tips,
Tidbits, Old-Time Folklore and
Humor of Interest to Hunters

North American Hunting Club
Minnetonka, Minnesota

HUNTING CAMP ALMANAC

Mike Vail
Vice President, Products and Business Development

Tom Carpenter
Director of Book and New Media Development

Teresa Marrone
Editor

Dan Kennedy
Book Production Manager

Heather Koshiol
Book Development Coordinator

BatScanner Productions, Inc.
Book Design and Production

ISBN 1-58159-057-1
1 2 3 4 5 6 / 02 01 00 99

PHOTO and ILLUSTRATION CREDITS

Featuring the cartoons of David Harbaugh, Richard Stubler and Richard Tomasic. Line art on pages 52, 75, 80 and 112 by Larry Anderson. Line art on pages 30, 91, 184 and 185 by Teresa Marrone. Drawing on page 37 by Jeff Boehler. Drawing on pages 40–41 by Chris Armstrong. All photos by article author except: cover onlay, and pages 9, 17, 93, 103, 115 and 145, Phil Aarrestad; pages 11, 151, 163, copyright 1999 PhotoDisc, Inc.; page 13, Tom Tietz.

Table of Contents

INTRODUCTION

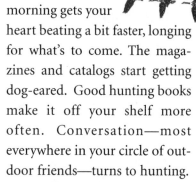

by Tom Carpenter,
NAHC Staff Member

As a North American Hunting Club member, hunting season is surely open year 'round in your dreams. Hunting magazines (like *North American Hunter* of course) and books, as well as outdoor catalogs, fill your nightstand, office, workshop, briefcase, magazine rack, couch-side stack, kitchen table, wherever … strategically placed to be available whenever you can grab a few moments.

But when summer starts getting along, your anticipation notches up a step or two. The bow or rifle makes it out of its case more often for trips to the range. An unseasonably cool morning gets your heart beating a bit faster, longing for what's to come. The magazines and catalogs start getting dog-eared. Good hunting books make it off your shelf more often. Conversation—most everywhere in your circle of outdoor friends—turns to hunting.

And then, finally, the time has arrived. You're hunting again! It's hard to believe it. Sometimes you have to pinch yourself to make sure, but … you're at deer camp again for the firearms season, greeting family and old friends and feeling good about the world once more; or maybe you're coming home from a day of bowhunting, bird hunting or small game hunting, wishing autumn could last a couple months longer.

No matter what the time of year, what you hunt or where you do it—wilderness mountains, faraway hills or plains, or woodlots and fields practically out your back door—you can always find a few odd moments to enjoy some little tastes of hunting. That's what the *Hunting Camp Almanac* is all about.

Leave this *Almanac* strategically placed in your home, take it to camp during hunting season, and just enjoy these short but fascinating tales, and snippets of lore and advice.

First you'll find *Traditions And Memories,* a special section celebrating hunting and the important part it plays in our lives. You too will recall partners and adventures of old when you read this—people and times that have made a difference in your life.

Then, in *These Are The Days,* you'll come back to the present and rediscover why life just wouldn't be the same without hunting as a part of who you are.

You'll also turn *An Eye To The Future* and discover stories and advice on "starting" young and first-time hunters ... and

you'll surely recall memories of your own first, great trips into the field.

Finally, to keep your skills honed, *The Fundamentals* provides insights into hunting equipment, strategies, skills and techniques ... real things you can take to the field to become an even better hunter.

It seems that life is extra-busy for everyone these days, no matter what stage of life you're at. That's just the way it is. But when those few spare moments become available, it's nice to have something like the *Hunting Camp Almanac* around, to take you away if only for a few minutes. And this book is 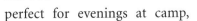 perfect for evenings at camp, when just a little reading will do before you drift off to sleep.

And, what the heck, we'll say it right here: This makes the perfect "outhouse" or bathroom book ... something you can pick up again and again and always find something interesting, insightful and maybe even a little educational to read.

Enjoy this *Almanac*—at home and at camp—again and again.

TRADITIONS AND MEMORIES

HONORING THE PAST

Hunting is very deeply imprinted in our memories. We seem instinctively to know the twang of the arrow, the snap of the bow; the sharp scent of gunpowder brings memories of crisp mornings afield and game in the bag. Our forefathers hunted for survival; today, most of us hunt for pleasure. But the tradition of hunting is still one of the most important things that is passed from generation to generation. We remember favorite places and the old friends with whom we shared special times, and honor the past by keeping those memories alive with our children.

A Letter To My Father

by NAHC Member Jacob VanHouten, Midland, MI

Dear Dad,

More than thirty years ago you gave me a life as a hunter, trapper and fisherman. Remember? I was six years old. It started that day you held the old Stevens .410/.22 over-under to my shoulder and let me pull the trigger. I hit that pop can dangling on a sumac bush not 20 feet away. The sound seemed like a cannon fire to my young ears, and I couldn't believe I had actually hit the can. I'll never forget that shot.

You taught me important lessons about gun safety. Like all young boys, I couldn't understand why you kept harping about it. You used to say, "More people are killed by empty guns than loaded ones." I didn't even understand what that meant. But I learned. I saw it in the papers and on TV. "A man was killed today as he was cleaning his rifle. Witnesses say the victim thought the gun was empty."

While you dressed me in my red snow suit to go deer hunting, you told me some of the secrets of where to find deer, how to hold still and how to keep warm. I remember your look when I said I had to go to the bathroom … five minutes after you had finished the 20-minute job of dressing me.

As I sat on our stand trying not to shiver too much, my lips blue, you'd ask me if I was cold. Too afraid to answer with the truth for fear of being taken home or, worse, left home next time, I would lie, of course, and say "n-n-n-o." You'd just smile and say, "Well, it's time to get going. Maybe we'll try a new spot."

I remember you waking us each morning of a hunt by hollering, "Daylight in the swamp!" I remember your Navy coffee that could start a diesel truck, made in the morning and heated again for dinner. I remember the "end of deer camp" dinner … any leftover food was thrown into a skillet, cooked and eaten. No complaints.

When I grew older and was able to push a trap spring down with my foot, you taught me how to make drowning sets for muskrats, dirt-hole sets for fox

and culvert sets for raccoons. You showed me how to run my trap-line and skin, flesh and stretch my catch.

You told me stories of how you and your father trapped together on the same stretch of Plaster Creek where I did too. You told me how you sold your first furs for Christmas money. I was following in your footsteps.

On camping trips you and Mom loaded five kids in a '63 Chevy station wagon pulling a trailer filled with gear and dragged it—and us—through Canada, Wisconsin and on the car ferry to Ludington. Any man who could do that, and live, can do anything. Maybe there *is* something to your claim that all those gray hairs came from us.

When I was 14 and able to rifle-hunt deer for the first time, you told me, "Don't be surprised if when you shoot your first deer, it doesn't feel so good and you feel let down. A deer is a large animal, and you might not enjoy the kill as much as you think." Every time I shoot a deer, I remember what you said that day.

I learned to respect nature. You taught me to track, to walk and run through the woods, to love hunting dogs, to enjoy the smell of fresh coffee on the camp stove, to pitch a tent in the pouring rain, to fish, to hunt and to cherish life.

Once I saw you broken down and depressed like I never had before. One of your closest friends had just passed away while deer hunting. You told me two things that made a big impression on me then, but they seem to become more and more relevant as I grow older. You said that Wayne had gone the way he would have wanted, and the way many people would want to go. You also said something that will stay with me always:

"You know, Jay, a man should consider himself lucky if he can count on one hand all the people he can truly call friend … and I've just lost one of them."

Well, Dad, I consider myself a lucky man … I count you on my hand of friends.

Members Write About · HUNTING CAMP

TAYLOR CREEK HUNTING CLUB *by James Gardner, Mildred, PA*

Our camp was built in 1938 by my father and my uncle and a few friends who lived in the town of Lopez, Pennsylvania. They started out with 25 members, and we still have 25 members today. We encourage the sons and grandchildren of the original

members to join. In the beginning it cost $50.00 to join—today it is $350.00. We still have the same bylaws they made when the cabin was built. We have made a few changes, but we try to keep it the same as when it was built, in memory of them.

I am now retired and go to the cabin almost every day just to sit on the porch and think about the days when we all hunted together. The hunting today is not like it was when I learned to hunt.

There's a spring by the cabin and we carry all our water. We start our deer season with a big turkey dinner and have a meeting after to discuss our hunting plans.

KODIAK'S CAMPS OF YESTERYEAR

by Gregg Gutschow,
NAHC Staff Member

K odiak. You can almost see the place without ever being there. Immense brown bears wading streams choked with salmon. Bald eagles coasting on air currents scanning for scraps. Sitka blacktails slinking along black sand beaches nibbling the salty kelp left behind by the tides. Whales, sea lions, foxes, otters ...

But for all these natural wonders, Kodiak is a hunter's dream inspired by one image—a hulking brown hear amid a tangle of alders. Big game rifles, compound bows and many other hunting tools have carried "Kodiak" model names because this island, and the bear that lives here, are widely considered big game hunting's ultimate adventure. Though most hunters will never go, most dream of going.

Even young Erik Ness, the young Minnesota boy battling leukemia who, a while back, became the center of controversy when he asked Make-A-Wish Foundation for a brown bear hunt on Kodiak. Despite the outcry from antihunting organizations, Make-A-Wish stood tall and granted Erik his dream hunt.

How does a teenage boy decide that a brown bear hunt on Kodiak Island is the epitome of big game hunting? Legend. And, somehow, the mystique of those old brown bear hunts and old brown bear hunters continues to be woven tightly into the fabric of North American hunting heritage. Maybe it's because we know that Kodiak still offers opportunity like it did back when Bill Pinnell and Morris Talifson started hunting the mighty brown bears.

Pinnell and Talifson are the primary characters responsible for Kodiak's bear hunting lore. From 1949 to the late 1970s, the duo outfitted and guided brown bear hunters from around the world. In fact, the top of the Boone and Crockett Club record book remains dominated by huge Kodiak bears taken during the 1940s, '50s and '60s. Their adventures inspired at least two books. Other men like Charles and Alf Madsen and Park Munsey were also brown bear hunting pioneers on Kodiak.

Giant bears still roam the lush Kodiak landscape, and bear hunters still come to Kodiak on guided hunts, but since Pinnell and Talifson retired from the outfitting business almost 20 years ago, the famous bear camps of yesteryear are being swallowed by the island and sea. Maybe that's not important. But, then again, maybe it tears at the fabric of Kodiak's legend just a little.

Take the Olga Bay cannery, which has been steadily crumbling into the Pacific. Pinnell and Talifson once called the cannery home, and used it as headquarters for their bear hunting business. The two got jobs as watchmen at the cannery in 1941. The job paid $150 a month, and the cannery was a palace compared to their previous cabin where they lived while mining gold and trapping otters and foxes. As their bear hunting business boomed, Pinnell and Talifson constructed small hunting cabins at other strategic spots around the island like Red River, Karluk Lake and Frazer Lake. Those camps, too, where so many tremendous brown bears were hunted, where so many thrilling hunts must have been recounted by the light of a lantern, are gone or fading into the landscape. They still brown bear hunt on Kodiak, but it's not like it used to be.

"There was a strong bond there (between brown bear hunters and guides)," says Dick Hensel, former Kodiak National Wildlife Refuge manager. "It was sort of a colorful period. The guides in those days were very cooperative with us and all had their own conservation ethic. They were supportive of our efforts."

Hensel added that many brown bear hunts conducted on Kodiak today are run out of

public-use cabins that are offered by the U.S. Fish & Wildlife Service, or tent camps set up by the outfitters.

Mike Fitzpatrick is a former guide who worked for Pinnell and Talifson from 1966 through 1975. "Old Bill was a bragger, but he always said one-third of the record-book bears were killed by hunters they guided," Fitzpatrick says. "They were real bear hunters, and Kodiak Island was home."

Fitzpatrick vividly remembers his first fall bear season on Kodiak. Twenty hunters paid Pinnell and Talifson to lead them to the famed Kodiak bears. All 20 harvested trophy browns. Following the 1966 season, more restrictive regulations were enacted to protect Kodiak brown bears. However, according to Hensel, these regulations were not a result of bear harvest on guide hunts. On the contrary, resident use increased dramatically and many of the bears taken by residents were sows. This, combined with illegal shooting of bears by ranchers attempting to raise cattle on the island, resulted in the more restrictive system.

Today, the Kodiak brown bear population remains strong. But 1966 might have been the last legendary year of brown bear hunting on the island.

It's a new era. The famed camps are gone, but Kodiak's still the place big game hunters can dream of.

Photo above: This tiny shack on Karluk Lake's Camp Island was used by bear guides and hunters decades ago.

Curtis Wolf

Hometown:	Oley, PA
Species:	Moose
Weapon:	.338 Winchester Mag, Federal Premium Nosler, 250 gr.
Hunting state:	Teslin, Yukon (Canada)
Guide:	Nisutlin Bay Outfitters

"This is by far the best hunt I have ever been on. Along with seeing all types of game—moose, caribou, bear—the scenery was breathtaking. I even managed to fish a secluded lake with my partner and caught some 5- to 10-pound lake trout. Upon leaving camp for home, by floatplane, I saw two moose fighting about one-half mile from camp. Both looked to be in the 65- to 70-inch class."

THIRD-GENERATION HUNTER

by NAHC Member
Cheryl Rude, Greenville, SC

I started hunting with my father and grandfather when I was 12 years old. Having children and moving away took me from hunting for some years but when our first son, Paul, was 12, he convinced us to try South Carolina deer hunting. It was certainly a big change from "going after deer" in my native California to "waiting for deer" in South Carolina. On one occasion I had a doe and a yearling come so close to me I could have almost touched them with my gun. It had been a doe day, but I had no desire to shoot.

In October 1997, I shot this 8-point buck. By 11 a.m. I had given up all hope of seeing a deer when all of a sudden he appeared right in front of me. Fortunately, he was more interested in his scrape than in fearing me. As he put his head down to move on, I slowly shouldered my rifle. I got a clean shot through the heart.

Hunting is a great family affair. While in his 80s, Grandpa Bert was still getting the trophy for being the oldest man in town to shoot a buck, and on the same day I shot my 8-pointer, my dad, Al Rist, shot a much bigger buck while hunting with my brother in Idaho. Dad is 85! 🖎

Old-Time Woodsman's Fire Starter: Fuzz Sticks

If you're short on tinder, make "fuzz sticks" by whittling slivers of wood partially off a dry stick that is about 10 inches long and about ½ inch in diameter. Leave the slivers attached to the stick, and make as many slivers as you can up and down the length of the stick. Arrange four or five fuzz sticks in a teepee shape, and light.

THE POSTER

by NAHC Member Tim Pengra, Northfield, MN

I t was a sunny Opening Day in the late 1950s. I was 8 or 9 years old, zigzagging like a dog through a large cornfield. Three huge roosters flushed as we neared the end of the field. They flew toward the Poster as he waited, shotgun in hand, for us to finish our walk. One, two, three, they dropped—hard! I ran to be the first dog there, retrieving the triple for the grinning Poster: Bud, my dad. It's there that my hunting passion started. The tradition had begun. We were quite a team. From that moment on, Bud had a hard time going hunting without me tagging along.

At 12, I got to carry a gun. On our first overnight trip together, we stayed at a farm on the shores of Mud Lake in western Minnesota. My dad's father had taken him there before WWII, a tradition they continued after Bud's discharge. We stayed in chicken coops cleverly disguised as hunting shacks. Since we had only one pair of hip boots, Bud carried me on his back across the sloughs. At night we gathered in the farmer's kitchen listening to gramp's old friends, former "market hunters," recall the good old days—remembering when.

For 38 straight years, the Poster and I took hunting trips together. To Canada, Minnesota, Iowa, North and South Dakota we traveled, holding licenses in each state at one time. Money was never an issue. It never mattered—we didn't have any, we just knew we were going hunting. Trucks, tents, campers, motels, and the homes of our friends—we stayed in them all.

Together we witnessed the marvels of Mother Nature at her best. The migration of the northern flight, seemingly endless against the Dakota prairie sky. In South Dakota, pheasants by the hundreds, sailing into a freshly picked cornfield as a winter storm approached. Snow geese in Canada, so thick it looked as though the farmer had laid down a white bedsheet to cover his crops. We saw it all.

The success of our trips was never judged by the amount of game we bagged, but rather by the laughs, adventures and camaraderie we shared with

think of all the places we've hunted, the great dogs we've had and the friends we've made. We sure have been lucky." We both nodded. We knew. Then the "remember when's" started.

We buried Bud the following summer. The Poster is gone,

our many hunting buddies. Last year's misfortunes became this year's laughs.

It was our last Opening Day in South Dakota. As we were driving to our spot, Bud turned toward me and said, "We sure have had some times, huh, Timmy? I'm just glad we got to do this for so long together. Just

marking the end of an era.

The hunting tradition with our friends will continue. On opening day, I will be the first to volunteer to post. As I walk to the end of the field, my thoughts will be happy ones, "remembering when." Who knows; maybe I'll even get my first triple.

DEER CAMP TRADITIONS
by various NAHC members

"Like most buck camps, traditions seem to evolve. Here are a few of ours:
- Newest and youngest hunters select their preferred hunting areas
- First buck killed, chops are consumed by the others
- All straight flushes in poker are labeled and tracked on the wall (a whole wall is nearly full)
- Any monies dropped from the table during a poker game cannot be picked up by anyone."

–Life Member William E. Duncan, Cedarville, CA

"We drive six hours from our home to get to heaven on earth. We always take plenty of chipmunk food with us. As soon as we park our motor home, the chipmunks run to their feeding rock. We put the food on the rock and then watch them play and eat from inside our RV."

–Life Member William Cooper, Bothell, WA

"One of the best traditions there is, is going out in the winter and bowling on the frozen pond; and walking to the cemetery of the family that originally settled the land (the last member of the family died in 1899)." *–Cheryl Cleveland, for my father Don Monks, Wellsboro, PA*

"Last year, our 11th season, saw three generations of family at deer camp. We eat well, play cards, tell stories and do some serious whitetail hunting. At our bow camp in October there's more canoeing, wood cutting and music playing than hunting."

–Thomas L. Warschefsky, Williamston, MI

" 'The Shack' sits on 40 acres in Northern Wisconsin. It has become a tradition in my family, not just for hunting but for family gatherings. My wife prepares every Thanksgiving dinner using the primitive shack kitchen with no running water, which has fostered a bond with our ancestors."
–*David S. Pearson, Washburn, WI*

"Our tradition is a trophy stein from Germany that is passed each year to the one in the family who gets the biggest buck."
–*John Hash Jr., Preston, MO*

"Our deer camp is located in the hills of Armstrong County, Pennsylvania, right next to the Allegheny River. No showers, lots of venison, long card games and hunting stories."
–*Michael Lucci, Parma, OH*

"One of the rules of camp is that the first one up in the morning turns the heater on and sets the coffee on top. The trick is to feed your hunting partner one more cup of coffee before he goes to bed, and then hold it longer than he can in the morning."   –*Lanny Olson, Puyallup, WA*

"It has been a tradition each year to toss jiggers of strong spirits into the fire as a tribute to friends and family who are no longer with us. The constellation Orion (the Hunter) gets a special salute, too. The few times we failed to pay our respects, we ended with no deer hanging from the meat tree. Coincidence? You be the judge."   –*Life Members David G. Koplar and Gerald Maher, Torrington, CT*

"...Sorry...I must have used my pheasant scent instead of my aftershave..."

The Easy Way To Skin A Squirrel

This technique works best when the squirrel is still warm. This technique works well even with field-dressed squirrels.

1. Starting from the underside of the tail, cut through the base of the tail-bone; leave the tail attached to the skin on the squirrel's back.

2. Use your fingers to loosen the skin over the spine for a few inches. Place squirrel on the ground on its back; put your foot on the base of the tail.

3. Pull upwards on both rear legs, peeling the skin inside-out all the way to the head and front legs. Keep your foot on the base of the tail.

4. Peel the skin over the belly and back legs, pulling toward the squirrel's back feet and finally over the ankles. Cut off the back feet at the ankle.

5. Make sure that the front legs are peeled past the "wrist," then cut off the front feet at the wrist. Cut off the head, leaving it attached to the skin.

6. Remove any glands under the legs (they look like small kernels that are darker than the meat) and clean the body cavity.

BACK HOME FOR BUSHYTAILS

by NAHC Member James Hart Isley, Lexington, NC

Turning off the blacktop, or as my grandmother used to call it, the hard road, I hit the gravel leading to a tiny, dilapidated homestead.

Even in the early-morning darkness I could see many changes. Lights from new houses along the way told me the land had been subdivided. What was once big woods was now landscaped yards. But I still recalled fond childhood days spent romping in that deep woods.

I parked the rental car where my grandfather's garage once stood, slipped on a canvas hunting vest and loaded my .22. Crossing the road, I searched the edge of what remained of the forest to see if I could find the trail my father, two brothers and I had long ago carved with frequent trips. Surprisingly, the faint path was still there in the undergrowth. I moved a few yards into the forest and stopped to let my eyes adjust. Even though it was very dark beneath the canopy of trees, memory guided me downhill to the stream I remembered from my childhood.

Soft rays of light wafted through the leafy branches to the east. It was the first week of September, and the Midwestern days were still hot and muggy. As I stood by the cool stream, listening to the trickling water and using my cap to fan away the heat and mosquitoes, I took time to get my bearings. The dim light made the setting look like a black-and-white photo, and I marveled at how little this section of woods had changed since my boyhood days.

A cool fog rose over the bottom-land as I stepped across the stream. I considered staying near the water, simply for the sake of comfort. But memories begged me to climb the hill on the other side to what was once one of my favorite squirrel hunting spots. As soon as I noticed the three familiar shag-bark hickories, I knew I had found it. My thoughts drifted back to days as a boy when my father would lift me onto a stump and I'd watch in wonder as he'd fill his limit of bushytails. It was an ideal place to hunt squirrels, and today showed great promise. I moved quietly, just as Dad had taught, edging myself the last few yards to that old, rotted stump that had somehow survived the years. I settled in to await the day.

As soon as morning light began to flood the forest floor, the woods came alive. *Whoosh!* The limber branch of a maple whipped skyward as a gray squirrel leaped from it onto a hickory limb. More movement told me the hickory was being used as a den tree. Small grays were scurrying about its limbs in all directions. As usual, the squirrels darted from spot to spot, making a clear shot almost impossible. I waited patiently for the right time. Scratching sounds of rustling dry leaves came from all along the hillside as the grays hit the ground to bury their treasures noisily.

The still air and warmth sent beads of sweat down my cheeks. Mosquitoes buzzed about, making it impossible to sit completely still. Nonetheless, it was a beautiful morning. The rising sun shot beams like lasers through the branches, drawing trails of golden light in the fog. Wake-up sounds of birds and animals evoked images of a spring turkey hunt.

Suddenly, there was the distinct bark of a fox squirrel as it climbed out to the tip of an oak branch and eyed me from 30 yards. Slowly I tucked the walnut stock of my Winchester lever-action under my chin, centered the scope's crosshairs just under the squirrel's ear, and gently squeezed the trigger. The sharp crack was followed by a soft thump, and the woods fell quiet. I ejected the empty casing and lowered the rifle.

It wasn't long before the forest came alive again. Soon the sound of teeth grinding a nut turned my attention to the high limbs of a hickory. Straining to find the source, I spied movement. Through the scope I made out the bushy plume of a tail; then the entire shape materialized. The rifle barked again; *thud,* followed by silence. There was a longer pause this time before the squirrels went back to work. But within two hours I had a small pile of bushytails at my feet. The heat was growing, so I decided to end the hunt. I stuffed the squirrels into my pouch and leaned back, deciding to linger a bit and enjoy my short time back in this place.

Taking a long look around, I let my mind wander back to summer days spent playing in these woods. I could almost hear the voices of children and even imagined my grandfather calling from the house with that funny "ya-hoo!" of his; dinner was ready. Those were good days, and this had been a wonderful place to be a boy.

I crept down the hill to the streambed, where I found a little relief from the stifling heat by dabbing cool water my on face. As I stood there taking in those familiar smells, listening to the buzz of insects and the bird songs, it seemed like the years that had passed between then and now had never been. It felt as though I was still that dirty-faced little blond boy in an untucked flannel shirt and patched jeans. Maybe, just maybe, if I'd call out softly, one of my brothers would answer from the next ridge. Although I considered it, I didn't call. It would have been too painful when no one answered.

Back on the road, I inspected the old homestead. The barn and chicken coop were gone, leaving only the smokehouse, the outhouse and the falling-down remains of my grandparents' home. Seeing the house that day— empty and rotting, the yard all grown over with weeds—one could hardly imagine what a bustling, happy place it had been. I gave thanks that I had known this place and that it had enriched my life with so many memories. I only wish my son could have a place like this to grow up in and to return to when the pressures of life begin to weigh him down.

With a sad smile I ducked into the car and slowly headed back toward the hard road. I've never gone back.

Old-Time Recipe File

Turk's Jerky Sticks

10 pounds ground venison (deer, elk, moose or antelope)
5 cubes beef bouillon, dissolved in small amount of water
1 ounce liquid smoke flavoring
⅔ cup Morton's TenderQuick
½ cup plus 2 tablespoons brown sugar
3 tablespoons pepper
5 teaspoons garlic powder
5 teaspoons onion powder

In large mixing bowl, combine ground venison, dissolved beef bouillon cubes and liquid smoke flavoring; mix thoroughly. In medium mixing bowl, combine remaining ingredients and stir to mix completely. Sprinkle the dry mixture over the ground venison and mix all together very thoroughly. Cover and refrigerate 12 to 24 hours.

Heat oven to 225°F. Fit a meat grinder with a small sausage tube, then run the venison mixture through the grinder. Cut to desired lengths and arrange on foil-covered baking sheet. Bake the jerky sticks 1 to 2 hours, or until dry. Store in refrigerator.

from NAHC member Randy Turechek, Cody, WY

"Roast mammoth…grilled mammoth…mammoth pot pie…mammoth soup…mammoth balls…mammoth-on-a-stick…next time I go hunting I'm going to kill a rabbit—period!"

Richard D. Owens

Hometown: Pinetop, AZ

Species: Mule Deer

Weapon: Remington 700 Muzzleloader,
               380 gr. Blackbelt Bullet

Hunting state: Arizona

"Some friends of mine in Montana, the Atchesons, have a motto, 'Hunt while you're physically able.' To that I'd like to add: Learn to enjoy and appreciate your time in the field, whether you're success-ful or not. And most importantly, share the experience with the kids; we need them."

COUNTY LINE CAMP

by Joseph M. Inglese, Amsterdam, NY

The camp I belong to is in the Adirondack Mountains of New York, in the town of Wells in Hamilton County. Our camp is unique in that it is coming up on its 77th anniversary.

The camp was started in 1922 by a group of men from Amsterdam, New York. Previous to that, the camp was home to a Civil War veteran. He had the building moved to its current location from a lumbering/tanning town called Griffin some three

miles away. Griffin no longer exists. We hold the title and deed to the camp and land directly from the Civil War veteran. In our region most camps are situated on leases from the big paper companies. The members on such leases hold no real ownership.

We are proud of our historical significance and that the founders set down bylaws that have helped keep the camp intact all these years.

These pictures show our camp as it looks today. The camp is called the County Line Camp as it is located along NY State Highway 8 not far from the Hamilton/Warren County line.

A TRIBUTE TO BEN LEE

by NAHC Member Nick Sisley, Apollo, PA

I f there was ever a woodsman who deserved the nickname "Big Ben," it was Ben Lee. Ben was certainly big in stature, but he was also as big-hearted as they come. His passion for the outdoors was without bounds. The outdoor world most certainly lost a legend when Ben Lee was killed in a car wreck in early October of 1991.

Ben's death particularly stunned me. I had hunted with Ben in South Dakota and took the last spring turkey that ever strutted in to his flawless calling. For that I feel quite honored and fortunate, yet I mourn his passing all the more.

On that South Dakota turkey hunt, I learned where you sit when hunting with Ben Lee. "Use this big belly as a pillow rest for your back," he'd say to new hunters.

Ben "talked" his hunters into bagging a bird. When he wasn't calling to the gobbler he'd be whispering to the hunter, giving him confidence, telling him how to do it, saying exactly where the tom was going to appear, getting the gun in exactly the right position. When the turkey finally appeared it was almost anticlimactic, for Ben had predicted the scenario to the final degree.

Ben Lee is largely responsible for spreading turkey hunting fever far and wide. Ben was to spring gobbler hunting what Fred Bear was to modern bowhunting. Ben Lee was one of the best turkey hunters this generation has seen.

Until 20 years ago, turkey hunting in the United States was limited to a few isolated pockets where bird numbers managed to hold their own. The art of turkey hunting, particularly calling, had been all but lost.

Ben Lee was one of the few masters, one of the keepers of the gobblers' secrets through those years when the tradition was nearly forgotten. Then as huntable populations came back, Ben Lee took it upon himself to teach a new generation of sportsmen the joys of spring hunting. He made

teaching it his life and his livelihood.

Ben never minced words. He told it like it was, even if it hurt, but there wasn't a malicious cell in his body. I'll never forget the first time we met. It was for a deer hunt near his home in Coffeeville, Alabama. Despite his 300-pound-plus size, Ben was as agile in the woods as Fran Tarkenton escaping an NFL pass rush. He walked with speedy purpose and never seemed winded. He could shinny up a tree as if he were 15 years younger and 150 pounds lighter.

When he had an audience in front of him, which was most times, Ben held it spellbound. Ben was always the same in front of a local sportsman's club, addressing an amphitheater filled with thousands or on television shows like "Today," "The Mike Douglas Show" and "Good Morning America."

Fellow outdoor scribe H. Lea Lawrence recalled hunting with Ben Lee and baseball great Ted Williams. Ben called in a turkey, Ted shot it and Lawrence wrote the story.

Ted and Ben got along famously for years, despite Ted's alleged brash personality. Ben could turn sarcasm right around. The two got together for spring gobbler hunts many times after the initial meeting, but Ted never hunted turkey again. Lawrence figured two things: Ted Williams simply enjoyed being around Ben and the excitement of hunting camp in April, and Ted wanted to be the best at whatever he did—and he knew intuitively he could never be a better turkey hunter than Ben!

Maybe Ben Lee's greatest attribute was generosity. He encouraged others to get into the turkey call business, then helped them do it right, despite the fact that he was creating his own competition. For the last years of his life Ben was associated with Wellington Outdoors. Wellington bought his call-making company, as well as Ben's name. Wellington used Ben's ability to charm audiences by scheduling him heavily on the seminar circuit.

Ben never had a college degree, never had any formal business training. His upbringing, insight and ability to solve hunting dilemmas somehow allowed him to bypass peripheral problems to cut right to the heart of the matter—an attribute he could have taught today's politicians and statesmen.

Throughout his life, Ben battled a weight problem. On that last spring hunt I noticed Ben breathing harder than I for the same effort. In prior years it was always the opposite with me envying how effortlessly he slid through the woods. So despite Ben being only 46 years old, his quick end was fitting. A "cutback" lifestyle never would have suited Ben Lee. He hunted and lived at 110 percent. The Lord threw away the mold when he made Ben Lee. And when Ben hit that bridge abutment, a once-in-a-lifetime hunting friend was taken from us all.

I never shoot a turkey without looking upward and giving thanks, and now I'll throw in a wink to that big, big man—my friend, Ben Lee.

Turkey Vision

One of the reasons turkeys so often elude hunters is their amazing field of view. A human sees an area of about 170 degrees without turning his head. A turkey sees approximately 275 degrees, and can easily see 360 degrees with the slightest movement.

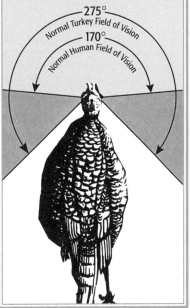

As the hunt progressed, Thag began to think Oog's new-fangled 'bow' might not be such a silly idea after all …

Useful Knots Every Hunter or Camper Should Know

The Transom Knot (right) is used to lash two poles or sticks together. This knot also works well to secure items to the luggage racks on top of your truck or car.

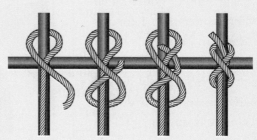

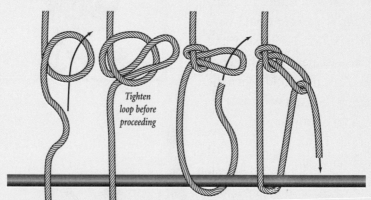

Tighten loop before proceeding

The Trucker's Hitch (above; also called the Power Cinch) provides a quick, pulley-like system. The end of the rope at the top of the illustration is securely tied off to a tree or other object. After the loop is made and tightened, the free end of the rope is wrapped around the object to be lifted, then passed through the loop. Pull down to lift or tighten.

BIG BEAR CAMP
by Joseph Stradel, Wayside, WI

Late 1930s. Grandpa Joe Stradel, far right

Grandpa Joe started hunting whitetails in 1923. This was a big hunt for a 16-year-old who had to ride a train 150 miles into the Wisconsin north. Some warned Grandpa never to hunt very deep into the woods because the remote wilderness was "hell country," and he would never come out alive. He hunted there anyway, bagging trophy whitetails.

When a tiny lumberjack shack was put up for sale in 1946, Grandpa purchased it. It was nothing fancy, but its location two miles off the main road made it the perfect place to hunt big whitetail bucks. He originally called the camp "Tipperary" after the World War II song. Then, in 1958, they changed the name to "Big Bear Camp" after my dad, Jay, shot the state record black bear (shown in photo at left).

Throughout the years and generations, we at Big Bear Camp have learned that deer camp brings a bit of heaven down to earth, whether it's the stillness of a bitter cold morning on stand, or the camaraderie and stories inside the shack.

Today's Big Bear Camp: Jay, Jeff, Joe and Jon

Grandpa has since passed away. Now Dad, my two brothers Jeff and Jon, and I enjoy deer camp. Soon we'll add nieces and nephews as the tradition continues.

• A PROUD HERITAGE •

Test your knowledge about the history of hunting and conservation

1. Where and when was the first U.S hunting license fee legalized?
    a. Pennsylvania in 1789, two years after gaining statehood.
    b. New York state in 1864; the license was for deer hunting,
       and the money was used to feed the needy.
    c. Wyoming in 1908, when President Teddy Roosevelt began
       promoting hunting in the Western states.

2. Wild hogs that roam the coastal states may be traced to:
    a. Hernando DeSoto and other Spanish explorers, who
       released hogs in the New World during the 16th century.
    b. Escaped barnyard hogs adapted to living in the wild.
    c. A herd of 50 wild boars that was released on a New
       Hampshire hunting preserve in 1893.
    d. All of the above.

3. The Boone and Crockett Club was founded by:
    a. Frontiersman Daniel Boone in 1821, a year before he died;
       the club was sustained by his grandsons after his death.
    b. Future U.S. President Teddy Roosevelt in 1887; he formed
       the club to help promote wildlife conservation.
    c. Dr. William Hornady, an eminent zoologist, in 1888; he
       founded the club to further appreciation of taxidermy.

4. Dr. Saxton Pope, one of the namesakes of the Pope & Young
    Club, was inspired to learn about bowmaking and shooting by:
    a. Legendary bowhunter Fred Bear, who befriended the
       young Pope in the late 1920s.
    b. A terrifying encounter with a bear, in which Pope success-
       fully defended himself with a sharp rock he tied to a stick.
    c. An Indian called Ishi, the last member of the Stone Age
       Yahi tribe, who was cared for by Dr. Pope in the early 1900s.
    d. Pope's mother Irene, one of the original Chisholm Trail
       Pioneers who learned the skill from Cherokee Indians.

5. When and where were the first flintlock muzzleloaders in use?
   a. Early to mid 1400s, in Italy.
   b. Late 1400s, in China.
   c. Early 1500s, in Portugal.
   d. Early 1600s, in France.

6. What caused the great decline in whitetail deer populations during the mid-1800s? *(mark all that apply)*
   a. Overharvesting by market hunters.
   b. Habitat loss caused by the pioneers' westward expansion.
   c. A massive infection of scurvy that decimated half the population over a 5-year period.
   d. Excessive logging, which depleted prime whitetail habitat.

7. What was the purpose of the Pittman-Robertson Act of 1937?
   a. It established the first seasons for migratory waterfowl.
   b. It established excise taxes on arms purchases; the funds were used to improve wildlife habitat and for research.
   c. It restricted market hunting of many wildlife species in an attempt to halt declining populations of whitetail deer.
   d. It established the first Wildlife Refuges and National Parks.

8. Who invented the A-5, the first auto-loading shotgun in production?
   a. John Browning, who sold the rights to Remington after a falling-out with Winchester.
   b. Eliphalet Remington, a blacksmith who founded Remington Arms Company.
   c. Arthur Savage, who also designed the lever-action rifle.

9. Where and when was the first archery-only hunting season held?
   a. Michigan, 1927.
   b. Wisconsin, 1934.
   c. New York state, 1940.
   d. Pennsylvania, 1945.

   Answers are on page 46.

William Strait

Hometown: Concordia, KS
Species: Whitetail
Weapon: Browning Bridger
               II Compound
               Bow, Easton 2117
               XX75 Arrow
Hunting state: Kansas

"I heard a noise coming through the timber. There he was, watching another buck with does. A fight broke out; I took the victor when he came into bow range."

"Learn to think like a bear…he went that way."

A Day To Give Dad Thanks

by Jeff Boehler,
NAHC Staff Member

Like at most Thanksgiving dinners, I'd eaten more than I should've. We'd arrived just that morning at my parents' home and enjoyed a feast with a roomful of family and friends. Football games, blaring from the TV, were the topic of conversation for the next few hours until it was time for leftover

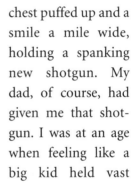

turkey and fruit salad. It appeared to be a carbon copy of past Thanksgivings but was, unfortunately, quite different. Dad, whose jovial, booming voice was normally heard above the rest of the crowd, was very quiet this day and looking years older than his late fifties. My dad, Adam Boehler, had been diagnosed with cancer just weeks before.

When the house grew quiet that evening, I perused a box of old photographs my mom had stored away. It was fun to see snapshots of old birthday parties, Christmases and family vacations. At the bottom of the box was an image I had long since forgotten. There in the living room of our old house was a freckle-faced, red-headed kid with his chest puffed up and a smile a mile wide, holding a spanking new shotgun. My dad, of course, had given me that shotgun. I was at an age when feeling like a big kid held vast importance and having my own shotgun meant I was well on my way to becoming a man.

Dad then introduced me to hunting. One early morning the next October he woke me from a deep sleep, poured me a thermos of chocolate milk, filled the lunch box with sandwiches and loaded me and my new shotgun into the station wagon. It was opening day of duck season.

The truck stop café at breakfast was filled with khaki hunting coats, the smell of fresh coffee, the sound of

TRADITIONS AND MEMORIES

35

bacon frying and the laughter of many happy hunters. At the slough, as we were gathering our gear for the day, Buff (short for Buffalo Bob) pulled me toward his car and filled both my shirt pockets with M&Ms. It was a memorable start to a glorious day.

I shot some teal that day in the big swamp and missed a bunch, but that was secondary. I was with Dad and his buddies, doing what guys do. Buff, a hulking man with pure white hair and a flat-top haircut, threw me up on his shoulder and carried me across the swamp to dry ground. Geno (Eugene) kept his black lab in the car after it wouldn't behave and the dog ate every one of his sandwiches, much to my delight. On the way home we stopped to replenish our shotgun shells and Geno put me on a saddle displayed on wheels and pushed me through the sporting goods store. That day kindled in me a spark for the hunt that has turned into a flame over the years. I owe my dad for that and for just caring enough to take me.

One magical day, Dad brought home a puppy for me. He had been battling Mom for months on the subject. "This will be a great dog for pheasants and grouse," he explained. "A boy needs a dog." Tanner, my new best friend, was a Visla—a Hungarian pointing dog and as beautiful a puppy as any boy could ever hope for. That dog was blessed with a great nose for birds and was at my side—or sometimes way in front of me—through prairie fields and cattail sloughs. One fall day, I screamed myself hoarse as he ran ahead flushing every pheasant in the county, miles out of gunshot range. But I shot a double on sharp-tailed grouse over that dog, and I cried like a baby the day he died. Thanks to Dad (and Tanner), I became a dog lover. A dog will always be part of our family, as Max, our Springer Spaniel, is now.

As I grew older, Dad taught me how to drive. When he learned how badly I wanted to hunt deer, he bought me a rifle for Christmas. As I was running around the track trying to win races, Dad was in the bleachers with a stop-watch. When I became an Eagle Scout, he was standing proudly by my side. When I rolled the Chevy off the highway, Dad was in the emergency room holding my arm saying, "Don't worry about the car," and "you're going to be fine, Sport," and cracking jokes to try to hide his worry and ease my pain.

That was twenty-some years ago, though it sometimes seems longer. We live half a day's drive away now and I've been busy with all the usual stuff. Our time together has been limited to a few holidays, scattered weekends and our occasional trip west for a week of fly fishing. Now that I'm older, I realize how much I owe him. I've also come to the humbling conclusion that I'll never truly be able to repay him. Even if he wins his battle with cancer and lives to be one hundred, I'll still be indebted.

When Sunday came and it was time to return home, I walked to the chair where Dad now spends most of his time. He stood and I gave him my biggest hug. "I love you, Dad," I said. "I love you too, Sport," he replied. And this time when I whispered to him "Thanks for everything"—I really meant it.

Author's Note:
My father never got the chance to read this story. Cancer took him from us two days before his 58th birthday, the day I had intended to show him these words so he could know how deeply I cared for him. I read it for him during his funeral service.

Actual early twentieth-century cartoon

Not Just For Teeth Anymore!

Ordinary toothpaste can come in handy for a number of hunting-related tasks.

• If your gun barrel or receiver has just a slight bit of rust on it, rub gently with a dab of toothpaste. Clean off all traces of the toothpaste, then apply a light coat of gun oil.

• Use toothpaste to break in the bolt of a new rifle, which removes the invisible factory roughness. As above, be sure to clean off toothpaste and oil lightly.

• Mint toothpaste makes a great hand cleaner. The abrasive action cleans grit, and the mint helps remove odors.

Richard Saliba

Hometown:	Dothan, AL
Species:	Alaska Brown Bear
Weapon:	Ruger M77-.338 Win. Mag, 250 gr. Barnes "X" Bullet (Handloads)
Hunting state:	Alaska
Guide:	Southeast Alaska Guiding

"The hunt was worth every penny. The guides (Mike and Hans) were super, the scenery was breathtaking and the game was plentiful. We saw more than 50 brown bears in 7 days. I would recommend this hunt without any reservations."

THE OLD HOUSE IN THE HILLS

by John Sloan, North American Hunter *contributing writer*

Nothing much happens in Rutledge. Once the bustling center of a huge plantation, it is now just the decaying remnants of time passing by. Only the old general store, though weathered and listing, showed signs of life. Rutledge is just a town that the wind blows through on its way somewhere else. It is here, just in front of the store, that the road to the hollow turns off.

I park near the neglected, weed-choked cemetery and pause, as usual, to tip my hat to Col. James C. Rutledge, 1800-1865, CSA, the late master of the old plantation. The wind moans through the naked branches of the huge oaks that shade the cemetery, and skiffs of snow scurry across the frozen ground as I move on again. It is, for lack of a better word, bleak. A winter day.

Frozen ground crunches under my heavy boots as I walk the trail into the hollow. From a turn, I catch sight of the roof of the old house. The old house in the hills. She stands at the edge of the grown field, looking out over the hollow. A notch in the hills lets the wind whine through her fallen chimneys and gush through the paneless windows. More than 150 summers have bleached her walls. The winters have tossed her shingles and peeled her

paint. For many years she has stood silent, alone. Gone are the kids and company that made her halls ring with laughter and music. Coon hunters say that on a still, cold night, they sometimes hear the plaintive notes of the fiddle and the ring of a banjo. They say only hunters can hear it. I don't know. I never have, but strange sounds ride the wings of the wind. This I know.

The bow rides lightly in my gloved hand. My right hand clutches a pocket handwarmer as I move past the house. I think of the yellow flowers that still fight their way above ground in the spring. I think of Col. Jim. I can see him coming home, dressed in tattered gray, limping from the pain of the mini-ball that still festered in his leg. There probably were few deer here then and even fewer some years later. The deer, the herd as it is now, is of recent vintage. These are new-comers with less than four decades to their lineage.

These recent arrivals to the late Rutledge Plantation are drawn to the area around the old house. In spring the fresh new growth crowds the fields. In summer the succulent green browse rings the old field edges. In autumn it is the choice acorns that come from the huge oaks and the opportunity for the does to be seen in the open but fallow fields. During the rut, they place themselves on display for the bucks that rub the young trees in the woodlines and make scrapes under the low branches of the beech trees. In winter, I'm not sure what draws the deer to this area and I'm not certain what attracts me to hunting this place, either. There's something.

I'm in the woods behind the house now. My pace slows and I pause often in the lee of big trees. The wind is bitter. I don't need to kill anything. In fact, I tell myself, I am not even really hunting. I'm just out and about. Just visiting a place that died.

Above me in a huge, old maple are decaying remains of

an old treestand. I wonder if a Rutledge built it. Nothing left but part of the board seat. Still, probably too recent for a Rutledge. They've been gone more than 30 years. Good place, though. In a beech tree to my left is a set of initials—CMR—that would be Charlie Rutledge, I suppose. I showed them to Jason once, and he said old Charlie must have been a hunter. I imagine him hunting here as a boy, maybe just a year or so older than Jason. It would be just as the deer started to come back to this part of the state.

Perhaps whoever built this stand was a bowhunter too. Perhaps he also missed a buck out of that maple. Maybe his broadhead is stuck in that hickory tree with mine. No, the hickory would not have been here then. The tree is less than 20 years old.

I stop at the edge of the woods. Across an abandoned, fallow field I see movement. A young doe steps from the far treeline. She is joined seconds later by another and then a third doe. They nibble in the frozen grasses. I could try a stalk, but most likely it would fail. Besides, I'm not really hunting.

They look sharply at the remains of the old orchard. Did they see something or did they just imagine a tree full of ripe apples? I've done that. Suddenly, all three deer look sharply toward the old house. Can they hear the singing or the ring of a banjo? Do they hear children laughing or the slam of a screen door? What is it about the house that has them worried? What can they know, these new-comers? The lead doe turns and walks stiff-legged back into the trees. The others follow. I notice that I have been holding my breath. Like a jump-started car, I begin to move again. What do the deer know that I don't? Why have they come here?

I cross the rock fence in a spot fallen down. I think, as I always do, of the slaves that built it—ancestors of Pop, now owner of the old store. Thoughts of Pop instantly remind me of the big pot of homemade chili he always has on the stove. Just 75 cents for a big bowl and all the crackers you want. I wipe my runny nose on the left sleeve of my jacket and circle back toward the old house and the road to the truck. I can almost taste the chili.

As I crest the hill, near the turn in the road, the wind gusts through the gap in the hills. I stop suddenly. Was it the wind in a treetop or was that a fiddle? I stand a minute. I can hear the clinking of a chain against the stone gatepost. Or is it the ring of a banjo fighting away the bleakness of a winter day a century ago? Perhaps an old servant playing while the women cooked and the men hunted. There were hunters aplenty then. Hunters such as I.

But then I'm not really hunting today. I'm just out and about. Maybe I just came to hear music. I'll have to tell Jason about this. We'll come in the late summer to place his stand in a tree. Maybe the maple. It will be his first year to hunt. Perhaps he'll be able to hear the music of the old house in the hills. ☙

Skunked!

If your dog—or heaven forbid *you*—gets sprayed by a skunk, here is a safe solution to eliminate the aroma.

1 quart 3% hydrogen peroxide

¼ cup baking soda

1 teaspoon liquid soap

Mix this solution when you are ready to use it, as it does not store well.

*—Compliments of **Wildlife Control Technology** magazine*

"Don't be silly—you don't get down from an elephant, you get down from a duck!"

Backwoods Meteorology
(or, There's a Bug in My Thermometer!)

Ask any old-timer the temperature on a summer's day, and he'll probably pause a minute before answering. Backwoods caginess? No, chances are, he's counting the number of cricket chirps he hears. Nature's smallest meteorologists have many ways of telling us the weather; here are a few you can use next time you're out hunting, fishing or camping.

Crickets are the most accurate insect thermometers. Count the number of chirps made by a common house cricket in 14 seconds, then add 40 to that number for the temperature. (Note: Crickets tell temperature in Fahrenheit, at least when you use this method!)

If the crickets in your neck of the woods are white tree crickets rather than house crickets, count the number of chirps made by one in a minute, then divide by four. Add that number to 40 for the current temperature.

Grasshoppers lose their voices when the mercury drops below 62°F, so if you hear the distinctive call of a grasshopper, you know it is at least that warm. If you see one flying (even if you don't hear it), it is at least 45°F.

Honeybees will remain in their hive until the temperature outside reaches 57°F. Bees outside the hive are most aggressive at temperatures below 70°F; as the mercury rises above that, the bees become mellower and less likely to sting. At 102°F, bees cluster outside the hive.

Ants won't be out and about until the temperature reaches 55°F; then, they'll come out and search for food (or whatever it is that ants do). When the temperature gets to 105°F, most ants will return to their tunnels; the exception is a species of ant in Arizona, which reportedly remains active even at that high temperature.

HUNTING CAMP ALMANAC

Boozed-Up Butterballs

4 orange-flavored prunes
4 shots whiskey
4 teaspoons orange marmalade
4 buffleheads, skin on
4 tablespoons butter

Marinate the prunes in the whiskey at room temperature for several hours. Drain and reserve whiskey. Heat oven to 375°F. Rub a teaspoon of the marmalade inside each duck and insert a prune. Tie each stuffed duck's legs together with kitchen string. Melt the butter and blend in the reserved whiskey. Brush the birds with this whiskey-butter mixture and place in a roasting pan. Roast 15 to 20 minutes for medium-well doneness, basting frequently with the whiskey butter.

from NAHC member Andi Flanagan, Seward, AK

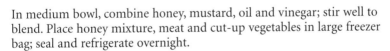

Marinated Elk Kabobs

⅔ cup honey
½ cup Dijon mustard
½ cup olive or vegetable oil
½ cup cider vinegar
1–2 pounds elk or venison steak, cut into 1–1½-inch cubes
  Vegetables: bell pepper, sweet onion, summer squash, etc. (depending on what is available), cut into same size as meat

In medium bowl, combine honey, mustard, oil and vinegar; stir well to blend. Place honey mixture, meat and cut-up vegetables in large freezer bag; seal and refrigerate overnight.

Prepare grill. Alternate meat and vegetables on skewers; grill until meat and vegetables are desired doneness, basting occasionally with marinade. Serve kabobs with wild rice or buttered noodles.

from NAHC member Larry Sawatski, Upper Darby, PA

1. *b.* New York state in 1864; the fee was $10.

2. *d.* All of the above.

3. *b.* Teddy Roosevelt hosted a dinner for prominent sport hunters after he saw the decimation of wildlife on his western ranch; he asked guests to join him in a club to preserve American wildlife.

4. *c.* The two men met while Dr. Pope was the curator at the San Francisco Museum of Anthropology.

5. *d.* Marin de Bourgeoys perfected the flintlock in the early 1600s; it remained the most popular muzzleloader until the early 1800s.

6. *a, b and d.* Market hunting was but one factor in declining whitetail populations. As pioneers cleared land for agricultural use, habitat was destroyed; logging further reduced prime habitat.

7. *b.* This act is also called The Federal Aid in Wildlife Restoration Act.

8. *a.* John Browning worked on the design of many Winchester guns, but refused to sell them the rights to his new self-loading shotgun due to a conflict over royalties. He sold production rights for the Browning A-5 to rival manufacturer Remington.

9. *b.* Wisconsin, 1934. Michigan and Pennsylvania followed 2 years later.

"Grampa Thog not use pointy stick, hunt cave bear with rock…great grampa Shug not use pointy stick, hunt giant sloth with rock…great-great grampa Moog not use pointy stick, hunt sabertooth with rock…"

THESE ARE THE DAYS

A CELEBRATION OF PRESENT-DAY HUNTING

Hunting is about a lot more than taking the life of an animal, or putting meat on the table or a rack on the wall. It's about the emotion you feel when your buddy nails that huge buck he's been working on all season, and you're there to congratulate him. It's about watching a flock of mallards set their wings over your decoy spread at first light. It's about hard work and the rewards that follow, and an evening spent with friends around the hunting shack's old woodstove, exchanging stories of the day's adventures. For hunters across America, these are the things to celebrate, and these are the days to remember.

THE DUCK BLIND

*by NAHC Member Tyler Holmer,
Plymouth, MN*

The golden sun slowly crept up from behind the small wooded area behind the duck blind and gave off just enough light to highlight the incoming ducks flying in the distance. The duck blind extended into the water and stared right up the middle of the figure-eight-shaped lake. Straight out from the duck blind lay two points, which extended out toward each other but did not connect.

Facing the blind, on the point to the right, sat three wooden, box-shaped duck blinds, with an open space in each of them from which to shoot. The powerful wind whistled as it hit on the right side of the duck blind.

On the opposite end of the lake, on a barren hilltop, a big red barn stood next to a tall white silo. The rolling hills of the surrounding farmland glowed with the dried-out, dark yellow crops of corn and soybeans. The few trees in the area stood tall, old and leafless due to the intense cold.

The decoy spread consisted of canvasbacks with red-brown heads and tails, black beaks and gray backs, and goose decoys with blackish heads and gray bodies. All of the decoys faced into the bitter wind and had icicles growing off the tips of their bills. The day was freezing, yet the lake still looked beautiful in the sunrise.

The duck blind seemed as if it might be a part of nature, as it blended so well with the rest of the lake area. It consisted of a green, L-shaped dock with camouflage walls disguised by golden-brown cattails. The blind must have been invisible to the eyes of the ducks. At the base of the dock sat a camouflage boat with an ice-covered bottom; the five-horsepower motor on the back must have been over fifty years old. Long, black barrels of shotguns lined up against the front wall of the blind, and empty red shotgun shells lay scattered all over the floor. Hawks squawked and bats sputtered in the trees behind the blind. A flock of geese slowly passed over the blind, making a loud honking noise; the air made a throbbing sound under the wings of the large birds. The bluebills' wing beats sounded like the buzzing of bombers as they roared over the duck blind. Finally came a splash on the water after the birds set their wings for a smooth landing to mingle with the attracting decoys. At this very moment, the duck blind proved to be a very beautiful sight to behold. 🖎

Don't Forget The Third Dimension

When you're shooting at a moving target, it's important to remember that not all shot arrives on target at the same time. The length of the shot string can help you hit what you are aiming at. Quality loads offer controlled shot stringing and pattern consistency to give you the best chance of hitting a speeding bird or clay. Knowing how a pattern strings out can help you in your wingshooting.

"He can't talk right now—he has a frog in his throat."

"Do me a favor...stop saying, 'At least we won't have to portage.'"

Who's Out There?

Old-time woodsmen claim that you can tell what sort of critter is peering at you from the woods at night by looking at the color of the eyes gleaming at you. Next time you're out in the woods, try to identify the eyes you see.

Bright orange eyes, closely set .... Bear
Bright yellow eyes, near the ground .... Raccoon
Light yellow eyes .... Bobcat
Bright white eyes, near the ground .... Fox or dog
Bright white eyes, in a tree .... Porcupine

Jeff Swinford

Hometown:	Fayetteville, TN
Species:	Rocky Mountain Bighorn Sheep
Weapon:	Remington 700 .300 Weatherby, custom-built by Jeff Swinford
Hunting state:	Colorado
Guide:	Al Valejo Outfitters, guide Loren Dillinger

"The hunt on Pikes Peak was a rugged, beautiful challenge. Al Valejo really knows where the rams are. My ram came out of a group of 17 rams. I shot the ram at 260 yards off Loren Dellinger's shoulder. It was so steep I couldn't use a rest."

A Perfect Elk Bowhunt

by NAHC Life Member
Larry Baca, Los Alamos, NM

On the opening morning of the 1992 New Mexico elk bowhunting season I was into elk even before it was light enough to see. Walking up a ski hill toward my hunting area, I spooked one off the slope. It was an encouraging start.

Later as I reached the top of the 10,200-foot mountain, I got more encouragement. Bulls were popping branches and banging antlers just over the ridge. After 45 minutes of maneuvering, I was in position for a 40-yard shot. My arrow found its mark in a 5x5 bull.

As I sat watching the downed bull to make sure it wasn't going anywhere, a brightly dressed hiker came up the slope behind me. I walked back down to let him know I had an elk down and was waiting for it to expire. I was uncertain of what the non-hunter's response might be; some people are pretty sensitive about such things. I was elated when he asked if he could watch with me if he was real quiet. A non-hunter wanting to be a witness—no problem!

I approached the bull cautiously with a nocked arrow, but it was over. Carl, the hiker, helped me position the bull so I could begin the cleaning chores. It was all we could do to unwedge the bull from the thicket of spruce and aspen it had fallen in and pull its hind legs downhill.

As I cleaned the elk, I explained the anatomy of the animal and what some of the body parts were. I told Carl about ivory and bugling. Sensing his genuine interest, I showed him the damage a razor-sharp broadhead could do. He was very appreciative of the lesson and equated dressing the elk to cleaning a fish. Well, close anyway.

After I finished, Carl asked, "What's next?" I told him I usually cut off what I could carry and took it back to my packframe, then began packing out the rest of the elk piecemeal.

He looked at the elk and said, "I bet both of us could drag it down the slope." I was hesitant, but I don't believe in looking a gift horse in the mouth. Over the tall grass covering the steep slope, we slid the bull down without much trouble.

About three-quarters of the way down, we stopped to take a breather. Another hunter, named Ron, approached and presented a rope from his pack, offering to help drag the bull the rest of the way. Could a hunt get any better than this?

The rest of the drag took as long as the first part because the slope became more gradual and gravity did less work. But very soon we were at my truck, positioning the bull for skinning and quartering.

Ron, who is a machinist, asked if I would mind trying a knife he had made from very hard steel and the antler of an elk he had taken the year before in Colorado; he wanted to see how it held an edge. My mom didn't raise any fools; I gladly accepted.

The entire skinning and quartering was done with just one touch-up with the steel I carry. Never before had I used a knife that made quartering an elk so easy. Ron helped me load the pieces in my truck. I gave him a ride to his truck and was home by 1:15 on opening day!

A non-hunter was educated about elk anatomy, learned the effectiveness of bowhunting and had his first experience dragging a bull elk. A fellow hunter exhibited consummate ethics and friendliness. I came home with enough prime meat to stock my freezer and a symmetrical 5x5 rack for the wall.

Can anyone top that as the perfect elk hunt?

Camp Recipe File

Cajun Venison Tenderloins

2 venison or other tenderloins from the day's hunt

¾ cup milk (canned milk works fine; dilute it a little before measuring)

1 egg

¾ cup all-purpose flour

4 teaspoons blackened steak seasoning*

2 tablespoons bacon grease or oil

1 small onion, quartered and sliced ½ inch thick

Slice the tenderloin into 2-inch lengths and flatten slightly by smacking with the flat side of your knife. Place in a bowl with the milk. Let soak 30 minutes.

In another bowl, beat the egg with 1 tablespoon water. Combine the flour and *1 tablespoon* of the seasoning mix in a pie plate or shallow dish.

When ready to cook, heat bacon grease in a skillet (cast iron works best) over medium heat. Remove a piece of tenderloin from the milk and roll it in the flour. Dip both sides in the beaten egg, then roll again in flour and add to the skillet. Repeat with remaining tenderloin pieces, working quickly so the first pieces don't overcook. Fry until the bottom side is browned and crispy, then turn the meat over and sprinkle with the remaining seasoning mix. Scatter the onions over the meat. Cook until the second side of the meat is browned and crispy and the meat is done to your liking. Tenderloin is best when eaten medium rare to rare; if cooked to well done, it will be tough.

*Use a commercial mix like Chef Paul Prudhomme's Blackened Steak Magic.

from NAHC member Teresa Marrone, Minneapolis, MN

RED BUS HUNTING CLUB

*by NAHC Life Member James Cummings Jr.,
Middle Grove, NY*

Our hunting camp is located in the beautiful Adirondack Mountains of upstate New York, near the little town of Speculator.

It was organized about thirty years ago with about ten members, most of whom still participate. The original camp was an old red school bus, hence the name "Red Bus Hunting Club." In the mid-1970s we were granted a lease by International Paper. That summer we erected the current camp, using the lumber from an old lumber mill barn. From then until now very few modifications have been made. We have no running water, no inside plumbing (which makes those trips to the outhouse in the middle of winter very quick) and a small generator for lights and television. We currently have 17 members with sleeping capacity of 21.

To use the word "member" to describe the guys in the camp is wrong. We are more like brothers. That includes the youngest guy at the age of 20 to the oldest, my father, who is now 82 years young. It does not matter what time of the year we go up to the camp; we always have a good time enjoying the outdoors and each other's company. Unfortunately for me, the U.S. Coast Guard has moved me to Hawaii, so last year was the first deer season I have missed up at the camp in 10 years. Luckily for me, my uncle (an original member) kept me informed of their success during the season via E-mail.

"Sports! Sports! Sports! Why can't you just hibernate like everyone else?"

The Measure of a Man

"What do you think those antelope's horns measure?" If you're like most hunters, you've been caught in the field without a tape measure more than once. But if you memorize the measure of your hand, you'll always have a quick, reasonably accurate measurement system, er, handy.

7½"

Here are some things to measure, and then remember:

• The distance between the tips of your thumb and forefinger, fully extended (as shown above)

• The distance from the tip of your thumb to the tip of your pinkie when your hand is spread as wide as it can comfortably go

• The length of your index finger, and the length of the first joint

Another handy measuring device you usually have with you is money. A U.S. dollar bill measures 6⅛" x 2⅝"; a quarter is just under an inch across (¹⁵⁄₁₆", to be exact); and a penny is ¾ inch across.

• JUST THE BEAR FACTS •

North America's bruins...of all types

1. Can a human outrun a brown bear?
a. Browns are very slow and lumbering, so a hunter in good shape can easily outrun one.
b. Browns run about the same speed as a human marathon runner, so you've got a good chance if the ground is flat.
c. Browns have been clocked as fast as 46 mph; don't even try.

2. If you are threatened by a bear, your best defense is to:
a. Run away as quickly as possible.
b. Act aggressively; wave your arms and shout, and try to make yourself seem as large and threatening as possible.
c. Climb the nearest tree and throw stones at the bear.

3. In good black bear country, bear population densities average:
a. Two black bears per square mile.
b. One black bear per square mile.
c. One black bear per two square miles.

4. Match up these common names with the correct latin name:
a. Grizzly bear   *Ursus maritimus*
b. Black bear   *Ursus arctos horribilus*
c. Polar bear   *Ursus arctos middendorffi*
d. Alaskan brown bear   *Ursus americanus*

5. Why are a polar bear's ears smaller than other bears?
a. Polar bears rely on the sense of scent more than other bears, so its ears don't need to gather as much sound.
b. Smaller ears are less likely to get frostbite or freeze.
c. Its ears are proportionally the same size as those of other bears, but look smaller because polar bears have thicker fur.

6. *True or false:* The liver of a polar bear is highly prized by Eskimos due to its rich flavor and fatty coating.

Answers are on page 98.

MY FIRST LONGBEARD

*by Tonya Brune (age 12),
New Haven, MO*

The first day of our hunt my dad (Paul) and I went to Unionville, Missouri. We heard a gobbler on roost but it flew off with some hens. Dad called the hens in and the gobbler followed. I had a chance to shoot it but I passed on the shot because we were filming with "Outdoors in the Heartland" and the camera couldn't see the bird when I had a shot at it. Then, when the cameraman *could* see it I didn't think it was a good shot so I decided to pass on it because I didn't want to make a bad shot and wound the bird.

The second day we heard some gobbling but couldn't get any birds to come in. On the third day we had roosted some birds the night before and we had a gobbler coming to us off of the roost first thing. It gobbled and gobbled and was coming closer. It almost made it to the point where I could shoot it and some cows in another field ran over to see what all of the commotion was about. I guess that scared the gobbler enough that he wouldn't call anymore.

We went back home, and on Friday when I was in school Dad shot a turkey. The next day Dad told me he would take me out to try and get me a gobbler. We went to a neighbor's farm to hunt where Dad said he had seen some birds the day before. We sat down and heard a little gobbling on roost but nothing close. We watched a gobbler and some jakes in a field in front of us but they wouldn't come in. At 6:55 that morning we heard a bird and he sounded pretty close.

Dad called, and the turkey gobbled back. Dad called again and this time the turkey triple gobbled. Dad told me to get ready because the turkey was coming in. I could hear him drumming so I knew he was strutting and getting real close. Dad whispered that he could see the bird, but I couldn't because a tree was in the way. The gobbler moved a little more so I could see it and I had a clear shot. Dad said shoot. I pulled the gun towards the turkey's neck and shot. The turkey went down. My gobbler weighed 23½ pounds, had 1¼" spurs and an 11" beard. I was so happy to have gotten a bird like this on the first Sunday of turkey season. Even if I hadn't shot a turkey I would still have had fun. Dad and I saw other animals in the woods and had a chance to enjoy nature's beauty. If you go hunting you don't have to kill anything to have a successful hunt.

Precisely Pattern Your Turkey Loads

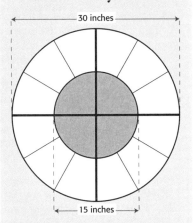

Core density is important in your turkey pattern. Before using this chart, you must determine your gun's point of impact. Then, center the point of impact on the crosshairs of the chart. Adjust your choke and load combinations until you find the combination that produces the most pellets in the center circle at 20 yards.

"Hi. My name's Tom, and this is my brother, Tom, and my other brother, Tom."

Packing The Grub Box

There are two schools of thought in packing the grub box for a remote camp. The first says that each meal should be carefully pre-planned, and exact provisions brought in. If this is your style, read through the recipes you'll be using and make a list of everything needed.

The second philosophy allows for more flexibility. With this method, you bring in basic provisions and cook whatever suits the mood of the hunters each day. The following list is a good starting point for a party of four hunters for five full days in the back-country. *Note: this list assumes that game (or fish) you take during the trip will be the major meat source; otherwise, plan on packing in frozen meat also.*

MEAT, EGGS AND CHEESE
Canned meats are heavy but can save the day if the game pole is still empty.

- 4 to 6 pounds bacon
- *Optional:* 4 to 6 cans tuna, Spam or dried beef
- 2 or 3 pounds jerky
- *Optional:* a small ham
- 4 pounds cheddar cheese
- 4 dozen eggs
- 2 pounds hard salami

VEGETABLES, STARCHES AND SIDE DISHES
Depending on the weather and the tastes of the hunters, you may also want to bring in salad fixings, cabbage, mushrooms and other perishable vegetables.

- 15 pounds potatoes
- 4 pounds carrots
- *Optional:* rutabagas, sweet potatoes, turnips, parsnips
- 3 to 6 cans tomatoes
- 2 or 3 pounds spaghetti or rice
- 1 box mashed potato flakes
- *Optional:* bagels, flour tortillas
- 5 pounds apples
- 5 pounds onions
- Oatmeal or other cereal
- 6 to 8 cans vegetables (corn, peas, green beans, kidney beans)
- 4 cans tomato sauce or paste
- 2 or 3 pounds elbow macaroni
- 3 to 6 cans baked beans
- *Optional:* dried beans or peas
- 3 pounds oranges and 1 lemon

DRY STAPLES
- 2 boxes biscuit mix (for biscuits, pancakes, breading, etc.)
- 1 or 2 boxes dried milk
- 2 to 3 pounds dried fruit
- Ground coffee, teabags
- 1 pound all-purpose flour
- 1 pound each white and brown sugar (more if party members use a lot in coffee, etc.)
- 4 to 6 loaves bread

SEASONINGS AND OTHER COOKING ESSENTIALS
- 1 quart vegetable oil (more if you plan on deep-frying)
- 1 or 2 jars mixed herb blends
- 1 bottle white wine vinegar
- 1 bottle maple syrup
- 1 or 2 jars jam
- *Optional:* pickles
- 2 pounds butter or margarine
- *Optional:* shortening for frying
- Ketchup, mustard, mayonnaise
- Chicken and beef bouillon
- *Optional:* soy and teriyaki sauce
- Salt, seasoned salt and pepper
- 1 or 2 bulbs garlic

Kevin Kendrick

Hometown:	Louisville, KY
Species:	Mountain Lion
Weapon:	PSE Bow, Easton 2312 Arrows, Vortex Broadhead
Hunting state:	Montana

"Hunting with top-notch NAHC members, in exceptional hunting areas, produces quality game. Thanks to this formula, I have a 174-pound trophy mountain lion."

"Our speaker tonight's gonna tell us how he made it through the last five seasons without ever seeing a whitetail…"

Just Plain "Pete"

by Jeff Boehler,
NAHC Staff Member

Hunting season was over. After two weeks of gray, cloudy weather the sky cleared up as if on cue. Glorious beams of sunlight shone through the stained glass windows to the south, warming those of us in attendance as I sat there remembering the first time I met my friend Lowell "Pete" Peterzen.

Less than a decade ago I had been invited to attend a sportsman's club that met weekly for lunch and a program on hunting or fishing. A promise of good food, tall tales and hunting stories was too good to pass up, so I went to a meeting of The Fur, Fin and Feather Club. Not knowing a soul there, I sat at a table with friendly-looking people, hoping to fit in. A robust gentleman offered me a firm hand and a genuine smile as he introduced himself as "just plain Pete." I instantly took a liking to Pete and ever since have sat at his table whenever I could.

Later that year, he invited me to see his trophy room I had heard so much about. Expecting to see trophies accumulated from Pete's hunts all over the world, I was not disappointed. Cape buffalo, elk, deer, mountain lion, caribou and grizzly bear were just a few of the many trophies tastefully displayed. He told stories of driving home from the Yukon with moose antlers tied to the camper's roof. He talked about the horses used on his elk hunt in the western mountains. But I could tell his favorite hunting stories were about the people he shared his campfire with, the guides who led him through wild places and hunters and trackers who he became friends with on the African plains.

And not one of his trophies created a sparkle in his eye like that when he showed me pictures of his family. There was no question what this man valued above all else. He talked proudly of each of his 12 kids (six children and their spouses); his ever-multiplying number of grandkids held a special place in his heart as well. And even after a lifetime together, when he spoke of his wife Lois, it seemed as if they were still high school sweethearts and were going on their first date,

or would be going to the prom together on the next Saturday or were still writing love letters to each other.

One spring, Pete entertained the Fur, Fin and Feather Club with a slide show and talk on his 30 years of big-game hunting. The standing-room-only crowd listened to his every word as he told tales of his hunting trips from Africa to Europe, from Alaska to Wyoming and many ports in between. Once again, his focus was not on the animals he pursued, but the people he had experienced these wild places with. His voice beamed and the audience laughed as he relayed humorous events.

His voice faltered and the crowd grew silent as he passionately remembered his hunting buddies that were no longer with us. Notably, the last slide was a photo that most of us in the room could relate to; we all have similar pictures tucked away in our photo albums. Pete said that of all the hundreds of slides he had taken over a lifetime of hunting, the image of him and his boys—at deer camp in northern Minnesota, decked out in head-to-toe blaze orange and set against a backdrop of snow and jackpines—was his all-time favorite.

So, this is how I remembered Pete as I sat in the full church on a November Saturday. Along with every other moist-eyed person in the congregation, I was there to celebrate Pete's life and his entrance into a place where there's surely a spot saved for him by the campfire. He was "just plain Pete" in the sense that "plain" is defined as genuine, true, honest or pure. But really, there was nothing "plain" about this world-class hunter, loving and devoted husband, proud and caring father and grandfather and true friend. We all will "just plain"miss him. ✒

THE LINCOLN LOG
by Tad E. Crawford, East Sparta, OH

H ow about this for a really neat hunt camp? I own 122 acres, mostly wooded (a great white oak woods) with a few acres of food plot. There is an actual prehistoric Indian burial ground there. The farm is one of the highest elevations overlooking Tappan Lake in Harrison County, Ohio. We've killed lots of nice deer there including two that just missed B&C and a few in the 140s and 150s. The "cabin," as I call it, is pre-Civil War (built before the time of Abe Lincoln), so I named it the Lincoln Log. It is an original dovetail log cabin, on its original site, and has yielded a news-

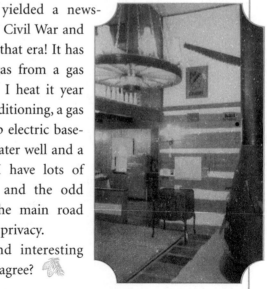

paper printed during the Civil War and even a family bible from that era! It has unlimited free natural gas from a gas well on the property, so I heat it year 'round. It also has air conditioning, a gas log fireplace (also backup electric baseboard heaters), a great water well and a few small fish ponds. I have lots of turkeys, squirrels, deer and the odd black bear. Being off the main road about a mile gives lots of privacy.

A most unusual and interesting hunting cabin, don't you agree?

How To Determine Windchill

If you're hunting in chilly weather, you need to take the wind strength into account as well as actual air temperature. This chart will help you determine the effect of the wind on your body's perceived temperature.

Wind Velocity (mph)	Actual Temperature (°F)									
	60	50	40	30	20	10	0	-10	-20	-30
	Equivalent Temperature (°F) Due to Windchill									
5	58	48	37	27	16	6	-5	-15	-26	-36
10	53	41	28	16	4	-9	-21	-33	-46	-58
20	47	33	18	4	-10	-24	-39	-53	-67	-81
30	44	28	13	-2	-17	-32	-48	-63	-78	-93
40	42	26	11	-5	-21	-37	-53	-68	-84	-100
	Little Danger				Increasing Danger			Extremely Dangerous		

5 mph feels like a very gentle breeze. At 10 mph, the wind is noticeable on exposed skin. Small branches will move at 20 mph, and snow or dust will swirl around. A 30-mph wind will move large branches and make telephone wires sing; whole trees will bend in a 40-mph wind.

"Gosh, I'm sorry, pal, but none of us know which way to get you back to the lodge either…"

THINGS THAT GO *BUMP* IN THE MORNING

by NAHC Life Member
Tony Anderson

While working for the Clearwater National Forest in northern Idaho, Terry Byrd and I decided to take advantage of a long weekend.

We borrowed some camping gear and headed into the remote Pete Ott Lake region. We each carried a pistol. Mine was a 9-shot H&R .22 rimfire revolver and his was a Ruger .22 rimfire semi-auto.

Early one morning I woke up to find frost on everything. We were high in the mountains, and I decided to go back to sleep and wait for the sun to warm things up.

I went back to sleep, but an hour later, something woke me. Because it was so cold, I had my head inside my sleeping bag, so I couldn't see what it was. At first I thought a chipmunk was scratching on my canvas-covered sleeping bag. I feigned sleep as the critter continued to scratch and nudge the bag. I could feel its slight movements on my back.

Suddenly I realized that those movements were a little too firm to be from a chipmunk. I listened carefully. Then I realized that something was *smelling* me!

The animal would nudge me, then sniff my back. I now suspected it was a wolf, since we had seen wolf tracks earlier.

I was on my stomach with my hand under my pillow; my .22 was near the pillow. Slowly I moved my hand until I could grasp the revolver.

With a firm grip on the gun, I spun around and hit the animal squarely with my elbow. Before I could see what I had hit, however, I sat face to face with a medium-sized black bear sow. Right beside her sat her cub, which I had just smacked in the head.

The cub, which was only about 18 inches long and looked like a big ball of fur, took off. That left me, the sow and my pip-squeak pistol. I aimed directly between the sow's eyes; only two feet separated the end of the barrel from her forehead. All sorts of possibilities flashed through my head. But most of all, I hoped she wouldn't attack, because I knew that my .22 pistol wouldn't deter the bruin.

So I did the best thing I could think of: I aimed to the side and fired a shot beside her ear. And then I hollered, with as much thunder in my voice as I could muster, "Get outta here, ya big *@∧#~*!!"

Well, that sow didn't flinch. She just sat there. And stared at me. Her eyes got bigger.

And so did mine.

It was up to her.

At that moment, I stood at one of life's peculiar crossroads where I had no say over which path I would travel. A short step and a quick swat from her front paw and I would be heading up that last quiet trail.

Then, out of the corner of my eye I saw movement. It was the cub. It had made it down to the lake.

Somehow, the sow also seemed to sense that her cub was out of harm's way. She stared at me squarely, then turned and loped down to the lakeshore.

That's when the adrenaline hit me. I stood up, pistol in hand, knees shaking and exposed—in my underwear—to the early-morning sunshine. I heard myself yell, somewhat belatedly, "There's a bear in camp!"

Terry, who was curled up in his sleeping bag, just laughed. "Bears won't bother you," he said, "they're just curious."

At that moment I would have paid a small fortune to have that sow stroll back into camp and stand a foot or two from Terry's sleeping bag.

My advice to fellow NAHC members who encounter black bear when they are not bear hunting? Use common sense. And carry a .44 Rem. Mag.—just in case. 🖎

"You seem familiar with the area. Were you born here?"

Pheasant Stew with Dumplings

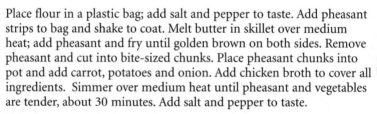

> ¾ cup all-purpose flour
> Salt and pepper
> 4 boneless, skinless pheasant breasts, cut into strips
> 1½–2 tablespoons butter
> 2 cups diced carrots
> 2 cups diced potatoes
> 1 cup diced onion
> Chicken broth

Place flour in a plastic bag; add salt and pepper to taste. Add pheasant strips to bag and shake to coat. Melt butter in skillet over medium heat; add pheasant and fry until golden brown on both sides. Remove pheasant and cut into bite-sized chunks. Place pheasant chunks into pot and add carrot, potatoes and onion. Add chicken broth to cover all ingredients. Simmer over medium heat until pheasant and vegetables are tender, about 30 minutes. Add salt and pepper to taste.

While stew is simmering, prepare dumpling dough, below. When pheasant and vegetables are tender, drop dumpling mixture by tablespoons into hot stew. Cover pot tightly and cook 15 to 20 minutes without lifting the lid.

Dumplings for Pheasant Stew

> 1 egg
> 3 tablespoons vegetable oil
> 2 cups all-purpose flour
> 2 teaspoons baking powder
> Pinch each of salt and pepper
> Milk

In mixing bowl, beat egg. Stir in oil. Gently stir in dry ingredients, and add enough milk to form a batter that can be dropped by the spoonful.

from NAHC member Joyce Good, Smicksburg, PA

Lynn Johnson

Hometown:	San Angelo, TX
Species:	Elk
Weapon:	Matthews Bow, Easton Arrow, Thunderhead Broadhead
Hunting state:	New Mexico
Guide:	Ross Johnson Outfitters

"After a night of heavy rain, opening day broke clear and cool. Just after daybreak this bull bugled once from across a valley. I was fortunate to catch up with him and his cows by around 8:00 and it took another hour following them to close to an acceptable shooting distance. At 65 yards I was as close as I was going to get. A fortunate shot made for a short but successful hunt."

BUCK FEVER: CAN YOU HANDLE IT?

by NAHC Member William J. Michaeli, Alpena, MI

Have you done your homework for the upcoming season? All of us hunters think about scouting before the season, but just how many of us get up out of that old easy chair and actually put forth the effort? This story is for all you armchair hunters. Sit back and let your mind feel the excitement of this hunt.

Imagine for a moment that you're in a treestand overlooking two trails that connect an endless hardwood and swamp to a freshly cut hayfield. You've been on stand for over two hours this evening. First you sit, then you stand. You end up with a bad case of the ups and downs. Treestands are not made for comfort.

It is now after 6:00 p.m. Your stand is on the shaded side of the field. The longer the shadows grow into the field, the farther out from the edge of cover the deer will creep. But so far, the only sounds you hear are those of an occasional bird or chipmunk.

Suddenly, you hear the faint sound of a branch breaking some 60 yards away up the trail to your left. Your head snaps in that direction and your heart starts to pound. IS IT?! COULD IT BE? Staring intensely in that direction, you see movement. A buck comes into full view only 40 yards out. Suddenly the tree you are in develops a massive case of "Buck Fever." The leaves on the upper branches start sounding like a rattler stuck in a cardboard box. It's the 8-pointer, the one with a 20-inch spread. It's the smallest of the three you've been watching all summer. Five yards behind him is the second buck, the 10-pointer with the higher and wider rack. This one could make 145, easy.

Their movements are slow but direct and the bucks are coming right toward your stand. By now the sweat has started to form on your forehead. Of all the times to be testing that new scent-lock suit you ordered from Gander Mountain in August! The first one passes your stand just 15 yards out, then the second one comes by. But where is the big boy—the 14-point non-typical that's always with these two?

174 P&Y buck by Bill Michaeli

Both deer have stopped at the edge of the field less than 20 yards away. You keep telling yourself to calm down, take long, slow breaths. Maybe this will slow your heart rate and stop the pounding inside your head. Because this is IT! The moment of truth … it's now or never.

Is the bigger buck still with these two? You try to decide if you should take one of them. Suddenly both bucks look back over their shoulder. THAT'S IT! The sign you've been waiting for. Sure enough, here he comes, closing the gap between you and destiny. The 14-point. OH MAN, HE'S **BIG**! At 30 yards out he stops behind a tree. Five minutes go by like hours. By now your heart feels like it's about to choke you. You keep trying to calm yourself and pray that he will not hear the drum in your chest.

All you are thinking about is PLEASE! Keep coming my way. Then without hesitation, in he comes. At 15 yards the buck stops again, in full view, broadside. You've been waiting for this your whole life. Countless hours of practice, scouting, watching and waiting are about to pay off. It all boils down to these few seconds.

You draw, anchor and drop the pin over the deer's vital area. You move your index finger back slowly to the trigger release. YOUR HEART IS POUNDING! You pull the trigger ever so slowly and send the arrow on its way. Everything goes into slow motion. Your dream is coming true, when suddenly you feel a tap on your shoulder: Wake up, dear! You were dreaming again, and it's time for dinner. Go get cleaned up and make sure you wash all that sweat from your face.

Damn! That *was* a dream? Why did you wake me up? Now I will never know if I got that big buck or not! After taking one last look at the man holding that 14-pointer in the magazine photo, you say to yourself, well at least that hunter's dream came true.

You know, some of the best hunts we've ever been on are right there in our minds. *Can you handle the excitement?*

WORLD'S FASTEST EVACUATION
FROM A HUNTING LODGE
BY FIVE HUNTERS, ...
JOINED FOR DINNER
BY TWO GRIZZLIES.
JUNE 10.

The Tale Of The Deer Track

It's not 100% reliable, but you can often determine if a track you see
was left by a buck or a doe. Here are some common clues to look for.

TYPICAL BUCK TRACK

Urine spray *ahead of* rear hoof print

Larger, deeper tracks; dewclaws
visible even on firm ground

Path with several turnarounds
caused by deer checking behind

Drag marks between tracks

Tips of hoof appear splayed

TYPICAL DOE TRACK

Urine spray *behind* rear hoof print

Smaller, shallower tracks; dewclaws
not visible except in soft soil or snow

Straight path with little or no
evidence of turning around

Clean line of tracks with no drag

Tips of hoof parallel or turning in

Your odds of successfully identifying the deer as a buck or doe will
increase when you see a track that has several of these characteristics.

IT SURE BEATS A LEAN-TO
by Nancy and Cort Manning, Northboro, MA

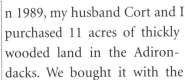

I n 1989, my husband Cort and I purchased 11 acres of thickly wooded land in the Adirondacks. We bought it with the intention of some day building a camp, but there never seemed to be enough money. So every spring we built a lean-to from small trees and tarps, and put tents under it. In summer we camped with our kids; in fall, Cort and his hunting buddies transformed the lean-to into "Deer Camp."

Little by little and tree by tree, we cleared a good-sized piece of land. Also, Cort started saving things. He helped a friend take down a porch and saved the windows. He helped remove an old deck and saved that too. Someone gave him a wood stove that was all rust and he refinished it. Our cellar looked like a flea market and held everything *including* the kitchen sink.

Each hunting season, the guys made the offer: If you need help building your camp, just let me know. In 1996, we called everyone on their offer, and each one came through. One weekend was spent pouring cement, one framing, one roofing, and so on. The weather didn't always cooperate, but our friends did. We finally had the camp that we had dreamed of.

Now we needed a name, but nothing seemed to fit. Then one day, a man came driving down our dirt road. He introduced himself as the former owner of the land. We invited him in to show off our camp in progress. As he was leaving, he looked back at our camp and said, "It sure beats a lean-to" and drove off. My husband and I looked at each other and knew we had the name for our camp …

FIRST HUNT: SPIKE TAKES ALL

by Jessica Weber,
NAHC Field Test Coordinator

I had many expectations about my first deer hunt. For instance, I expected it to be cold and boring. I also expected it to be stressful because my dad was planning to sit in the stand with me on opening day, so I knew there'd be no backing out—I'd have to shoot if we saw a deer. Plus, I knew I had better not miss or, worse yet, simply wound a deer because I'd hear about that forever (my family can be rather relentless when it comes to this type of thing).

Although most of the members in our party were veteran deer hunters, I wasn't the only rookie; my cousin Zachary was also going deer hunting for the first time, which helped take some attention away from me. On Friday afternoon everyone arrived at the cabin and scurried about finishing up last-minute tasks. Later that evening a dollar was collected from each hunter—this pot would go to the person with the biggest buck on opening day.

Saturday morning finally arrived. As Dad and I walked to our stand, we laid down a scent trail in hopes of enticing a buck. Our heated deer stand, combined with unusually mild weather, made it easy to stay warm and comfortable. Then came the hardest part of deer hunting: waiting. We sat in silence for about two hours before we started to hear shots in the distance; this made me more anxious to see something, anything! About 30 minutes later I suddenly heard some rustling to the left of our stand. It was a good-sized spike buck standing 100 yards away! As it followed the scent trail we had laid earlier, my dad gave me the signal that I should get ready to shoot.

Carefully and quietly, I got the deer in the crosshairs of my .243 rifle. But just as I was about to fire, the buck moved. I thought that I had blown my chance for sure, but luckily the buck moved into position again. I found the buck in my scope, aimed, took a deep breath and fired. The buck fell to the ground, then jumped back up and ran into the woods.

I turned to my grinning dad and with a squeaky voice said, "I'm shaking like crazy!" He replied "Me too!" We were both very excited!

Before this experience, I had imagined that when you shot a deer it just fell over and died right there, so when my buck ran off into the woods I feared I had only wounded him. Even though Dad reassured me that the shot had been lethal, it was difficult to sit and wait before following up the shot. In between looking at my watch, I prayed that the deer was really down. I dreaded the thought of disappointing my dad and being tortured by the rest of my hunting party—this year and every year to come.

Finally it was time to climb out of the stand and look for my deer. All my fears were put to rest when we found the deer about 15 yards from the point of impact. CELEBRATION! Dad pulled the deer into a clearing where we field dressed it.

By the time we got the buck loaded into the pickup and arrived at the cabin, most of the hunters in our party were back—and everyone else was empty-handed! At noon it was looking as if my spike buck might be the winner of the "Big Buck contest." This made everyone determined to beat me in the afternoon hunt.

After lunch, my dad and I went back out to the deer stand, but the pressure was off for me, so it was more enjoyable. Just as the sun went down, a nice doe walked out in the field about 200 yards away from our stand. Though we waited for a buck to follow, it became evident we had to shoot the doe now or it would be too dark. I wanted to see my dad in action, so I told him to take the doe. He shot and the doe ran off into the nearby woods. Because it was getting dark, we immediately walked across the field and tracked it a short distance into the woods, where we dressed it. That evening back at the cabin I was still the only hunter with a buck. My first hunting trip was not only exciting and successful; it was also profitable!

• BIRDS OF A FEATHER •

Waterfowl and upland game birds

1. When setting out a large number of goose decoys, it's best to:
   a. Set them in small clusters or "family groups" rather than spacing them out evenly.
   b. Set them two feet apart, as evenly as possible, so they look like a larger flock.
   c. Divide them evenly into two rectangular groups, and then conceal yourself in the space between the groups.

2. Ring-necked pheasants are originally from:
   a. India.
   b. Turkey.
   c. China.
   d. Thailand.

3. Which if the following statements about the vision of wild turkeys is true? (mark all that apply)
   a. Turkeys see with great clarity, but have poor color vision.
   b. Turkeys can see things toward the back of their heads.
   c. Although turkeys have excellent visual acuity, their depth perception is poor.
   d. Turkeys see poorly at night, and this is one of the reasons they nest in trees.

4. Which of the following statements about blue and snow geese are correct? (mark all that apply)
   a. Blue geese are a distinct species from snow geese, but they can interbreed.
   b. Lesser snow geese travel in flocks much larger than those of greater snow geese.
   c. Juvenile blue geese have a dark body and a white head.
   d. Snow goose populations are increasing to the point of collapse, as there are more birds than their tundra breeding grounds can support.

5. Which of these quail species attains the largest size?
   a. California quail
   b. Gambel's quail
   c. Mountain quail
   d. Scaled quail

6. Categorize each of the following ducks as either a puddle duck (dabbler) or a diving duck.
   a. Gadwall
   b. Redhead
   c. Ring-necked duck
   d. Pintail
   e. Goldeneye
   f. Widgeon

7. What is the fastest a mourning dove can fly?
   a. 25 miles per hour
   b. 40 miles per hour
   c. 55 miles per hour

8. Which of the following statements about turkey beards is true? (mark all that apply)
   a. The filaments that form a turkey's beard are the same compound that forms a deer's hooves.
   b. Only mature gobblers have beards.
   c. 20% of wild turkey gobblers have two beards.
   d. A single gobbler can have as many as nine beards.

9. If you've got a Hungarian partridge in hand, you can distinguish a male from a female because:
   a. The male has bright orange cheek pouches.
   b. Males have feathers between their toes.
   c. Males have a dark brown horseshoe mark on the breast, which is absent or much lighter on females.

10. *True or false:* To escape threats, chukar partridge prefer to explode into flight because their habitat has little ground cover.

11. *True or false:* Unlike other upland birds, forest and prairie grouse usually will not start another clutch if their first is destroyed.

Answers are on page 98–99.

THESE ARE THE DAYS

DON'T COUNT YOUR TURKEYS BEFORE...

by NAHC Member Max Brown

Wild turkeys are my favorite game. I have hunted them for about 15 years, killed about twice that number and still cannot get enough of it.

On this particular sunny April morning, I had followed the familiar ritual of getting into the woods an hour before first daylight. But by 9:00 a.m. I had neither seen nor heard a turkey.

I happened to have a new cedar box turkey call that my cousin had given me, which was supposedly given to him by the maker, so I decided to take a walk and work with the call.

After about a quarter mile, my practice was disturbed by a loud gobble coming from over a hill overlooking the field. After analyzing the situation, I decided to enter the woods on an old logging road and hide in the ditch within range of the field.

I got comfortable and repeated the yelps that had brought the gobble—with immediate results. Two gobblers answered, but by now they were out in the middle of the field. I raised myself up enough to see the gobblers, accompanied by three hens, walking in my direction from about 500 yards off.

A few minutes later, the turkeys had halved the distance and were moving toward me around the edge of the field. I pointed my shotgun down the road toward the field, planning to shoot the first gobbler that came into view.

Five, ten, fifteen minutes passed, but no turkeys appeared. Thinking they were probably still a few hundred yards away, I slowly lifted myself until I could see most of the field. Not seeing any turkeys, I stood up.

That's when the five turkeys, which were then about 30 yards away behind a weed patch, saw me. They ran away too fast for me to get a shot off.

I sat back down and waited for the adrenaline surge to go away. I tried a few notes on the call and was immediately answered by a gobble from the field. I didn't move but continued to call. The same two gobblers were answering me—and getting closer.

A few minutes passed. The turkeys continued to answer my calls but seemed to be stalled in the same spot as before. This time I was ready for them. Putting my gun to my shoulder, I pressed the safety off. Without making a sound, I slowly got to my feet while crouching over to keep the weeds between me and the birds.

When I straightened up, the turkeys saw me and began to run away as before. I took aim on a gobbler's neck and pulled the trigger. The bird rolled over, and I ran into the field to grab it.

Holding the beautiful bird at arm's length, I estimated the weight at 15 pounds. A two-year-old, I thought. The beard was about six inches long. I inspected the bird to see where it was hit. Curiously, I could find no shot holes and only one drop of blood on the neck. Good, I thought. This young gobbler would be fine for the table.

Laying the bird aside, I put my gun down while I removed my coat to unzip the game bag. Just as I got both arms halfway out of the sleeves, a blur of motion caught my left eye. It was my turkey, up and running for the woods.

Giving chase while shedding my already half-off coat, I covered about 20 yards before the turkey spread its wings and completed its exit by soaring over the tall pines at the edge of the field. My gun was back where I had been when the race started. I walked back to my caller, put it in my pocket and left. I had enough of matching wits with the turkeys for that day.

"I thought the reason they could see so far was that they had good eyesight!"

MUSK OX HUNT CLUB

by Life Member Terry Receveur,
Collegeville, PA

The cabin and headquarters of the Musk Ox Hunt Club is located off the Wabash River on an oxbow lake in Sullivan County, Indiana. It is directly adjacent to the Club's hunting area, which consists of 3,000 acres of leased land and riverbottoms. The club gained its name from an experience I had in October 1984.

While bowhunting that particular day, I was positioned on a very heavily used trail leading through some blackberry and honeysuckle thickets when I heard some barking dogs coming toward me. Having hunted in southwestern Indiana where wild dogs are common, I knew the dogs were probably running a deer. I readied myself for the emergence of a deer and hoped to get a decent shot. Sure enough, I soon heard a loud crashing sound. I looked in the direction of the noise and saw something coming toward me. At first I couldn't make it out. It was extremely large and had a very thick mane like a lion. My first thought was, "It's a musk ox!" As the thing neared I could see that it was a monster buck with a bird's nest tangle of vines and brush draped over its head and neck. The dogs had evidently run the buck through some pretty thick cover. I could tell the buck had a huge rack, because

even through all the brush I could make out long thick tines. Since that fall of 1984 we all knew the area held a monster buck, which came to be known as the "musk ox buck."

When we formed our club to provide rules and regulations governing the leasing of the hunting property, we decided that the club would be known as the "Musk Ox Hunt Club" in honor of the area that the musk ox buck called home. Over the years the hunting property has yielded some nice bucks, including a 165⅝ typical shot by Tim Receveur in 1993. However, rumor has it that the musk ox buck is still out there.

The biggest tradition is simply friends and family reacquainting. Since I moved away from Indiana in 1987, I have continued to make the annual trek back from Pennsylvania for the shotgun deer hunt. The reunion with my dad, brother and good friends is a cherished tradition.

As in many deer camps, a friendly $5-wager for the biggest buck (antler size) always instigates some friendly ribbing and reminiscing. Another tradition is our Saturday night dinner. Each evening after the Saturday opener, the group of five smelly hunters (we have no running water) makes the short trek into Illinois to enjoy fried catfish at a local diner.

It's A Weird, Wild World

from Keeping Track

North American Hunting Club members venture into the woods and fields for numerous reasons. From hunting to nature watching, they spend hours outdoors learning more about nature and the game species they pursue. Some of the things they see in these wild places border on the bizarre.

Take, for instance, the ruffed grouse that shares the Pennsylvania countryside with NAHC member Bruce Etchison. The bird greeted Bruce and his party at their camp during a spring visit. The friendly grouse was there on their return trips during the summer months and was following them into the woods like a young pup by the time deer season rolled around. If it wasn't walking along behind them, the bird liked to perch on an extended arm or finger.

Bruce affectionately tagged the grouse "Gertie." The bird followed him to his treestand one early morning and eventually flew up and joined him on stand. Gertie began making an annoying scratching noise up in the stand as it pranced around helping Bruce keep watch for deer. When Bruce attempted to encourage the grouse to find another location by pushing it over the edge, the grouse flew around the area and returned to land on Bruce's gun barrel. Deer hunting that day was frustrating at best.

On another trip the grouse followed Bruce more than a quarter of a mile to his ground blind. The feathered one entered the blind and promptly perched on Bruce's gun barrel.

An even stranger creature might be the buck that was killed by a vehicle in eastern Minnesota and recovered by NAHC member James Peterson. While

Minnesota white-tailed deer are famous for growing massive racks, this buck will make you do a double-take.

The buck grew a nice 6x6 rack but apparently wasn't quite finished since it grew another complete antler on one side, inside the primary rack. This second antler begins where the brow tine would be located on a typical antler. The addition is a very respectable antler in its own right, and the total Boone and Crockett score of this maze of antlers grosses 171²⁄₈. It took four scorers to determine which beam to use as the main one for scoring, since the twin beams are connected at the base.

From grouse that act like pups to bucks that grow unusual antlers, NAHC members seem to be finding truly wild specimens when they venture afield. Makes you stop and wonder about the "natural" world! ✍

John Shafron

Hometown:	Youngstown, PA
Species:	Whitetail (Non-typical)
Weapon:	Ruger .300 Mag, 180 gr. Winchester Fail Safe Bullet

Hunting state: Pennsylvania

"I saw the buck in bow season and thought about it day and night. After very patiently still-hunting, I bagged him on the second day of gun season. I felt a great sense of accomplishment."

—R. STUBLER—

"Get ready, Fred—I think we're going to see a bear!"

MULEY DOUBLE IN THE HIGH SIERRAS

by NAHC Life Member John C. Damman, Lake Hughes, CA

For the past 20 years, I have been packing into the Sierra Nevada Mountains in northern California for deer camp. It takes about eight months to plan a trip. The biggest and most important thing is having a good hunting party, made up of four or five guys who like to hunt for a week. You need to figure out where you'll hunt and who will pack you in. After that, there are lots of details to attend to: grocery shopping and packing everything into panniers; gathering and packing the camping equipment; and finally weighing all of this so you know how many mules you'll need to haul everything to your deer camp.

Let me share a High Sierras hunting story with you; I hope it gets you excited enough to try this type of hunting sometime.

The alarm went off at 5:00 a.m. The air was still and crispy, and the stars and moon were starting to fade with the rising sun. My buddy Jonsey was the first one up, so he built the fire and got the coffee brewing. He roused us all with the call, "Come on boys, the coffee's done and the bucks are jumping." We crawled out of our warm sleeping bags for breakfast, then put on our hunting gear. The air was still calm and and there was frost on the ground.

Jonsey and I would hunt together, with the others hunting in the same direction. I loaded my .300 Savage, Jonsey his .270 Remington, and we started across the meadows. As we approached the other side, I picked up some fresh deer tracks. I could see each hoof print in the white frost. There was more than one set of tracks, and I was sure they were buck tracks.

I motioned to Jonsey to come over and take a look, and we decided to track the buck down. We planned to stay about 150 yards apart and work our way up the hill following the tracks.

I'll tell you, tracking a buck muley in the High Sierras is work, but the thrill that goes with it sends chills up your back. I expected to see the deer with every step. As I worked my way up the mountain my steps were right on the buck's tracks. For over an hour, I followed the tracks: uphill, then downhill, around in circles and even zigzagging. At one time I thought I had lost it. Several times I had to stop and study the tracks to figure out which way it went. But with the frost still on the ground and a little luck, I picked up the buck's track again. With each step I looked ahead trying to spot this clever buck.

Chills went up my back as I suddenly came across some fresh droppings. It felt as if the buck were looking right at me. I continued up the mountain, taking one step at a time. Jonsey and the others were out of sight but in the area. Then all at once, it all happened. I froze in my footsteps as I realized I was being watched by a large mule deer.

I raised my rife to my shoulder. My knees were starting to shake as I focused the scope on the buck. As I squeezed the trigger, the buck started running. At that same moment another large muley jumped up. I ran up the hill trying to locate the spot where the buck had been when I shot, but I saw neither deer nor blood. For a moment I thought I had missed the buck, but the shot was only 100 yards at the most so I figured I must have hit it. As I started to backtrack my steps, I spotted it. I had bagged my buck on opening day! When I got to the spot I counted the buck's rack: 4 and 3.

I jumped with joy as I began to field dress the buck. But the hunt was not over. As I was tying up my buck for the drag back to camp, I heard the crack of Jonsey's .270 rifle. I then heard Jonsey cry out, "Hey John! Over here!" As I looked over to Jonsey's location, I could see that he had shot the other big buck.

I left my buck and ran over to see his buck. Jonsey had also bagged a nice 4-point muley. Then we both jumped with joy. I helped him clean and prepare the buck for the drag back to camp. By this time the rest of the hunting party had arrived and helped us drag both of the deer to our camp.

When we arrived at camp, we hung the bucks on a deer pole in the trees to give them a good cleaning, and then wrapped them both in deer bags. What a day it was.

Over the past 20 years we have taken some very nice mule deer home with us. We've also all gotten skunked a few years. But I can tell you that you'll never forget your deer hunting trip—when you live as we do for a week in the High Sierra Mountains at 10,000 feet.

"Uh, on second thought, Ed, maybe I will borrow some of that insect repellent you've got…"

Joe Evancho

Hometown:	New Stanton, PA
Species:	Moose (B&C score 219⅝)
Weapon:	7mm Magnum, 160 gr. Nosler Partition
Hunting state:	Alaska
Guide:	Dennis Reiner

"Third time is the charm. After two unsuccessful self-guided hunts for moose, I booked a hunt with Dennis Reiner of North Pole, Alaska. My dream came true, just south of Anatuvak Pass, with a 65½-inch wide, heavily palmated monarch that placed very high in SCI International and B&C 3-year record books."

• ALMANAC DEER QUIZ •

Test your knowledge about deer hunting

1. Nontypical antler growth is caused by: (mark all that apply)
   a. Poor weather in the spring.
   b. An injury to the buck's body, particularly leg or genitals.
   c. An injury to the pedicel (the base of the antler) during very early growth stages.
   d. Age and genetic history of the buck.

2. What is a good way to locate mule deer bucks? (mark all that apply)
   a. Look for their scrapes near sparse stands of timber.
   b. Glass from a high ridge in the morning, and work your way downhill.
   c. Start in a ravine or other low spot early in the morning, and still-hunt to higher elevations.
   d. Stand-hunt in a location between feeding and bedding areas.

3. What is the possible life span of whitetails that are not hunted?
   a. Bucks may live up to 10 years, while does have a shorter lifespan due to the rigors of birth.
   b. Bucks may live up to 10 years, while does may live over 20 years.
   c. Bucks and does both may live up to 15 years.

4. Which factors help develop trophy-class bucks? (mark all that apply)
   a. The mother was robust when the buck was born.
   b. The buck is getting high-quality forage.
   c. The buck is not pressured by hunters or other factors.
   d. Maturity: bucks over 8 years of age are more likely to have trophy racks.
   e. Genetics: trophy bucks often produce trophy-potential offspring.

5. If a whitetail buck lays both its ears back and widens its eyes, it means:

    a. It is trying to pinpoint the source of a sound.

    b. It is displaying dominance or aggression, usually toward another buck.

    c. It has spotted a receptive doe, which it is trying to lure in.

    d. It is deferring to a larger, more dominant buck.

6. Which of the following will a smaller buck do to show its subordination to a dominant buck? (mark all that apply)

    a. Tuck its tail between its legs and bend its back so its stomach is lower.

    b. Lick the face and forehead of the dominant buck.

    c. Wag its tail to show it's not in the mood for a fight.

    d. Make a low grunt and drop its nose to the ground.

7. In areas with high doe-to-buck ratios:

    a. Bucks don't make or visit scrapes as often as in areas with fewer does.

    b. Bucks make more scrapes to advertise their presence.

    c. Breeding success will be poor, because young bucks won't be able to breed as many does as older bucks.

8. When estimating racks in the field, use the ears as a guide in judging antler length. Typical whitetail bucks' ear length is:

    a. 5 to 6 inches long.

    b. 6 to 8 inches long.

    c. 7 to 9 inches long.

9. *True or false:* During the velvet stage, a buck's antlers are extremely warm to the touch.

10. *True or false:* If part of the pedicel of a deer is surgically removed and re-attached to another bone in the deer's body, it will develop an antler.

    Answers are on page 99.

MICHIGAN TENT CAMP
by Mart Van Stee, Kentwood, MI

My camp is in Huron National Forest, on government land in Alcona County, Michigan. We just concluded my 51st consecutive camp (I am 78 years of age), interrupted only by two years of service in WWII. Our crew consists of my son, Marshall, his two sons, Jay and Chris, my son-in-law Bob, his son Rob, and me. This year, two friends came along as guests.

We employ no guides, relying solely on our memories and compasses. Our camp always has been a "tent" camp, and each member helps with chores. Our main tent is large, with a conven-

tional wooden door and a barrel stove; personal gear is stored in a smaller tent. This season, during a big snowfall, the smaller tent's ridgepole broke and was repaired with the trunk of a young tree.

After the day's hunt, we have our main meal and build a campfire; good-natured bragging and fibbing are the order of the day. Well after dark, when the weather is right, the northern lights are fabulous—a dazzling display of color and motion. In the stillness of the winter's night, creatures of the forest present a cacophony of screeches, howls, and screams … all music to a woodsman's ears.

"Put Red Fred In The Shed"
(Or, How To Use A Baseplate Compass)

Sounds like a child's game, doesn't it? Actually, using a baseplate compass is easy enough that even kids can learn how; in fact, this skill is standard fare for Boy Scouts across America today. But many hunters never learned how to use this intimidating-looking gadget. Here's a quick lesson.

Take a look at a baseplate compass. You'll see a large arrow on the baseplate (usually interrupted by a magnifying lens). This is called the "direction-of-travel" arrow. Next, look at the actual compass dial. You'll note a floating

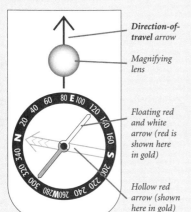

Direction-of-travel *arrow*

Magnifying *lens*

Floating red and white arrow (red is shown here in gold)

Hollow red arrow (shown here in gold)

needle that is red (shown here in gold) on one side and white on the other. The red part of the arrow—referred to as "Fred"—points north, which means, of course, that the white part points south. Finally, you'll notice that the outer ring of the compass can be turned, and that there is a hollow red arrow (again, shown here in gold) that rotates with the ring. This hollow red arrow is called "the shed" because it looks like a little house.

When you're in the field, choose a landmark to walk toward. Hold the compass straight ahead of you; the direction-of-travel arrow should point at the landmark. Rotate the ring of the compass (not the baseplate, just the ring) so the hollow red arrow lines up with the red part of the floating arrow (shown at right; remember, red is shown as gold in this illustration). Congratulations! You've just "put red Fred in the shed." Look at the number on the ring to determine the compass bearing you must travel; in this case, it is 140°, which is southeast. Now, even if you lose visual track of your landmark due to thick woods or hilly terrain, you will eventually reach is as long as you travel steadily on a 140° heading.

Land-*mark*

TWO TOO-CLOSE CALLS

*by NAHC Member
Dennis Woelffer*

During a 14-day sheep hunt with fellow NAHC member Greg Williams, who runs Nahanni Butte Outfitters in the Northwest Territories, I almost lost my guide, Al Baruir, twice to the perils of the wilderness.

Four days into the backpack hunt, Al spotted a herd of 12 Dall rams a mile off. We camped that night at the base of the mountains where he had spotted them. The next morning we walked up the mountain, found the rams and stalked within shooting distance.

My .270 Winchester and 130-grain bullets brought down a 39¼" curl ram at five o'clock to cap off a successful stalk. That night and the rest of the next day, we caped out the ram and rested.

On the seventh day, we headed out for our base camp. Al thought we should make it back to camp in two long days. But it proved a little harder going than we had hoped.

After two and a half hours of hard walking, we were getting close to the bottom of the mountain where we had shot the ram, when Al stepped on a rock and it gave way.

He reached up to grab a stick so he wouldn't fall down the cliff, but that stick pierced his hand, going two-thirds of the way through.

I was helpless because I couldn't get down to him, and he was only holding on by the stick jammed through his hand. The pain showed on his face as he pulled himself up to get a grip on the ledge with his other hand. He worked his whole body back up to safety but was in agony from the stick going through his hand. Hurriedly, we worked our way down to a river, where we washed Al's wound and bandaged it the best we could; but it was apparent that we quickly needed to get back to base camp and medical attention.

We crossed the river and headed for the top of the mountain on the other side. Al said that once we got there and found water, we would camp for the night.

In another two and a half hours, we made the mountain top and started looking for water.

It was close to 6:00 p.m. and we were eager to make camp. We headed for a spot Al knew would have water.

Suddenly, Al stopped and pointed to my left. "Look over there," he half-whispered, half shouted. For a split second I froze. To my left, 30 yards away, a grizzly bear was running parallel to us.

Al threw down his pack and grabbed his ax. He hadn't brought his gun on this hunt, so that was his only defense. While he was doing that, I loaded my gun, keeping an eye glued on the bear. I forgot to take my pack off.

Our hopes of the bear running off didn't come true. As it rounded a little clump of brush, it headed straight for us. As I prepared to shoot, the bear stopped and stood on all fours. Al told me to wait as the bear stood up for a brief second.

He barely got the words "Don't shoot!" out of his mouth, when the bear got down on all fours and headed straight for us. Al started shouting and waving his arms at the bear.

As it turned out, that helped save our lives because the bear ran at him instead of me. I was able to get a broadside shot at the bear's head as he passed a couple yards to my right. The big grizzly went down and never even twitched. I hit him right below the ear.

We paced off the shot after it was all over and after our hearts slowed down to a normal beat. That bear was only eight yards from where I stood as I shot, a little too close for comfort.

In two days we were back at camp, where Al caught a flight to the hospital. It turned out that his hand was not infected and would work as good as new. Al assured me he would never go out again without a gun.

As for me, my .270 did the trick, but I'm sure glad I had another change of underwear for the trip home.

Hunter's Recipe File

Chili Beans

  1 pound ground venison
  1 large green pepper, stem and seeds removed, diced
  1 large onion, diced
  2 (16-ounce) cans kidney beans, drained
  1 pint home-canned tomatoes, or one 14.5-ounce can tomatoes
  1 cup mild salsa
  8 ounces mild pickled peppers, drained
     Chili powder, salt and pepper to taste

In skillet, cook venison, green pepper and onion over medium heat until meat is browned, stirring occasionally to break up meat. Drain excess grease if necessary, and transfer mixture to slow cooker. Add remaining ingredients to slow cooker; stir well. Cover and cook on LOW heat for 2 hours. Serve hot.

from NAHC member Tim Roberts, Ballard, WV

Camp Cook's Clean-up Tip

If you're cooking over an open fire, rub liquid dish soap over the bottom and the outside of your pots and pans before putting them over the fire. The soot that accumulates from the fire will wash off easily.

"She wants to know if she could borrow some of our buck lure."

Steve Bruggeman

Hometown:	St. Paul, MN
Species:	Quebec Labrador Caribou (349⅜ P&Y)
Weapon:	Browning Bow, Easton Arrow, Thunderhead Broadhead
Hunting state:	Quebec
Guide:	Sammy Cantifio, Ungava Adventures

"This bull was taken near Ungava Bay in northern Quebec. There the Korac herd is nonmigratory and there are always caribou present, but never in the huge numbers that can be encountered in a migratory area. This is spot-and-stalk hunting from huge freighter canoes that travel the many bays and inlets where the tide is up to 30 feet every day."

NO PLACE LIKE HOME
by various NAHC members

NAHC members call a variety of structures "home" when deer season rolls around. Here are a few different ones we've heard about...

"A dozen NAHC members hunt free of charge from this 45-year-old Adirondack deer camp. The Bluffs door is open to any other NAHC member who cares to join us."
–Roger Sullivan, Ogdensburg, NY

"This photo is of our hunting camp in Wells, Nevada, on Ruby Mountain. It was a cold fall and to be successful during the hunt it was important to keep dry and sleep warm after a long day of hunting. So remember: Keep the fire-wood stacked up and the stove burning." *–Wayne Culberson, San Jose, CA*

"We are in our third generation at the 'Straw Deer Hunting Camp' in northern Minnesota. Early camp consisted of a ridge pole lashed between a couple of trees; one or two trucks were parked just right so a piece of plastic could be stretched over the toppers and the ridgepole. We now have 4x4 corner posts, precut 2x4s for structure and precut 1x4s for the roof. We can set up in about two hours."
–Marty L. Straw, Big Lake, MN

"My camp can best be described as 'spartan!' I hunt out of an old truck camper with propane heat and lights. On a good night, I can get the camper up to 50° at best. But it beats the back of a pickup! Heck, who needs all the comforts of home? When you're hunting whitetails, *that's* all you need!"
–Gary Shore, Kenmore, NY

"My deer hunting camp is a 1956 Ford bus. We have hunted in the same area, north of Aikin, Minnesota, for 41 years. This old bus has gone with us for 21 years. It has an electric refrigerator, gas stove and oven, and a forced-air LP gas furnace. It sleeps four people very comfortably."
–Melvin Hladky, Minnetonka, MN

"We've hunted whitetails with the 'Blue Goose' in northeastern Wisconsin for 19 years. During hunting, we live by the motto: The woods is our home and the wind is our comb."
–Jerome Bolle, Manitowoc, WI

"We started hunting Michigan's Upper Peninsula in 1964 and stayed in the back of a '58 Ford pick-up. Over the years we upgraded to tents, then travel trailers and finally, what you see here, 'Camp Mossy Horns.'" –*Life Member Dale Overbeek, West Olive, MI*

JUST THE BEAR FACTS Quiz Answers *(from page 57)*

1. *c.* Brown bears are capable of short bursts up to 46 mph, so you shouldn't try to outrun them.

2. *b.* Most bluff charges will be stopped by these simple tactics.

3. *c.* One black bear per two square miles.

4. *a.* Grizzly bear: *Ursus arctos horribilus*
    b. Black bear: *Ursus americanus*
    c. Polar bear: *Ursus maritimus*
    d. Alaskan brown bear: *Ursus arctos middendorffi*

5. *b.* Smaller ears are less likely to get frostbite or freeze.

6. False: the liver of a polar bear is poisonous, and is never eaten.

BIRDS OF A FEATHER Quiz Answers *(from pages 76–77)*

1. *a.* Small clusters or "family groups" look more natural to geese.

2. *c.* Ringnecks are originally from China; other pheasant species are from China, Japan or Mongolia.

3. *b, c and d.* The eyes of turkeys have many cone cells, which provide excellent color vision; therefore, *a* is false. Their range of vision is 300°, but they have poor depth perception and night vision.

4. *b and d.* Blue geese are simply a color phase of snow geese, so *a* is false. The body of a juvenile blue goose has large amounts of white, which turns darker as the bird matures.

5. *c.* At 8 to 9 ounces, the mountain quail is the largest of these species. Gambel's quail weigh 5½ to 6½ ounces; California and scaled quail weigh 6 to 7 ounces apiece.

6. *a.* Gadwall: puddle duck   *d.* Pintail: puddle duck
    b. Redhead: diving duck   *e.* Goldeneye: diving duck
    c. Ring-necked duck: diving duck   *f.* Widgeon: puddle duck

7. *c.* 55 mph; if you're missing them, you may have an excuse!

Birds Of A Feather answers *continued*

8. *a and d.* Keratin is the substance that makes up turkey beards, deer hooves and human fingernails. Hens can also grow beards, so *b* is false. Only 2% of gobblers sport multiple beards; the record is 9.

9. *c.* Male Hungarian partridge are easily identified with this marking. Prairie chicken roosters, not Huns, have orange cheek pouches.

10. False; although chukar cover is sparse, the birds prefer to run rather than fly.

11. True.

ALMANAC DEER QUIZ Answers *(from pages 88–89)*

1. *b, c and d.* There is some debate about the cause of nontypical antlers, but these factors are generally considered prime causes.

2. *b and d.* Mule deer don't make scrapes, so *a* is false. It's best to hunt mulies from above, since the deer expect danger from below.

3. *b.* Females typically outlive males, who are more stressed by the rut.

4. *a, b and e.* Pressure *per se* has no effect on antler development, so *c* is false. Bucks over 8 years are usually in the decline of their antler growth, so *d* is false.

5. *b.* This is a classic "challenge" pose, and may signal the start of a fight.

6. *a and b.* Deer wag their tails when they are content, so *c* is false.

7. *a.* In areas with high doe ratios, bucks may not need to advertise to find receptive does.

8. *b.* Adult whitetail bucks' ears are 6 to 8 inches long. Mule deer ears, by comparison, are typically about a foot long.

9. True. The velvet is filled with blood vessels which carry nutrients to the developing antlers.

10. As strange as this sounds, this has been proved to be true.

Bob Buriak

Hometown:	Williamstown, NJ
Species:	Eastern Wild Turkey
Weapon:	11-87 Rem SPS Turkey Gun, Federal Premium Turkey Load
Hunting state:	Indian Mills, NJ

"I would first like to say that I'm a handicapped hunter. I have spina bifida and walk with crutches. So I would like to say to all you handicapped hunters: Keep it up! I was hunting on a friend's blueberry farm about a half hour before daylight and got this tom gobbling for 1½ hours. I used every call I had—slate, box, yelper and mouth. Finally three hens came five yards from me and the gobbler 40 yards, and that was all she wrote."

AN EYE TO THE FUTURE

THE NEXT GENERATION OF HUNTERS

Remember the carefree days of youth? An afternoon spent plinking tin cans with the .22 down by the creek … squirrel hunting in your grandpa's back woodlot … getting up early to have breakfast with your dad before he went to his tree stand on opening morning of deer season? If you remember those days fondly, the best way to experience that special joy again is to take a young person—boy or girl—hunting. Not only will you be introducing them to the wonders of the outdoors and helping them build a skill that will last a lifetime, it's guaranteed to make you feel young again.

PASSING ON THE TRADITION

by NAHC Life Member Scott K. Johnson, Hubbardston, MA

Have you ever caught yourself wishing you had a son to whom you could pass on the ancient tradition of hunting? I once did, until my three daughters taught me differently. From day one, my daughters have been surrounded by the wonders of nature and the bounties it has to offer. They have endured and enjoyed my hunting expeditions and have accompanied me on numerous occasions.

We live in the north-central part of Massachusetts where large tracts of land are still underdeveloped. It is common for our family to drive around at dusk scanning the fields for wild game—mainly turkeys and white-tailed deer.

The girls have their own binoculars and are sometimes able to stalk within 50 years of deer when the animals first appear in the fields in spring. It is a game for the kids to try to sneak (talking and laughing as they go), as close as they can.

There was one instance when a mature doe stood her ground as her offspring from the previous year fed behind her. The doe even walked toward the girls in an attempt to threaten them away. It worked. The girls yelled back to me that the doe was coming after them. I told them not to worry, but they came running back to the car anyway.

During the summer I practice shooting my bow every night after work. My two older daughters, Keri, 9, and Robin, 7, each have their own compound bows. Leanne, 4, has a makeshift bow with a wooden arrow and does her best to keep up.

As fall approaches, the girls sense my enthusiasm for the upcoming archery deer season. They anticipate our weekend walks through the woods looking for "our" hunting spots. I try to show the girls what deer eat and where they bed. Keri and Robin tell me the names of wild plants as they collect them for their science projects. They explain to me that the plants provide nutrition for the animals. Our time together in the woods

is a good learning experience for all of us.

The past archery season the girls and I had placed two treestands in the woodlot on a private farm near our house. One stand covered the southeastern trail leading from a small oak grove and the second overlooked a trail close to a bedding area.

On the second Saturday of the season the wind was blowing from the northwest so I decided to take the stand covering the southeastern trail leading from the oak grove. It was mid-November and the rut was in full swing. Several small scrapes surrounded the oak grove and a rub line marked the trail toward the bedding area.

At daybreak I rattled antlers for five minutes, then waited and listened for ten more. The squirrels were out and about, so I rattled for five more minutes. I hadn't even put the horns down when I heard a deer approaching at a steady pace. I grabbed my bow.

The deer appeared at about 30 yards. Its head was low and it was coming in at a steady walk. Its route would place it directly below me for a five-yard shot. I drew my bow when it passed behind a hemlock tree.

As the buck quartered away from my treestand, I released an arrow, which caught the buck behind the left shoulder blade. The deer bolted and disappeared into the woods.

The blood trail was heavy and it didn't take long for me to find my prize—a nice spike buck with 11½-inch spikes. I left the deer where it had fallen and went to get the girls.

When I got there, my wife Karen and daughters Robin and Leanne were home. Keri was at a sleep-over at her friend's house and wouldn't be home until after lunch. I told the family that I had hit a buck and needed their help tracking him. They were ecstatic. They dressed in record time, and soon we were off on another outdoor adventure.

I pointed out the trail to the girls, then Karen and I stayed back and watched Robin and Leanne track the buck.

Robin lead the expedition with Leanne picking up the rear. They talked to each other as they progressed, saying, "Here's some blood!" and "There's more over here," until Robin finally yelled, "Here he is dad, over here! We found your buck."

I have never experienced such joy as watching these two future hunters ply their trade. Robin and Leanne went to the buck and lifted the head, admiring the animal.

The next lesson for them was to watch the field-dressing. They studied the procedure with amazement even after Karen told them they didn't have to watch if they didn't want to.

"We want to watch," Robin said. "When I get older I'm going to hunt with Dad." Leanne nodded her approval. Words cannot explain the emotions that surrounded this moment.

At the local deer registration station the deer weighed 127 pounds. While tagging the buck, the station manager asked the girls if they, too, were going to hunt when they got older.

Robin replied yes, and that they had helped Dad find this buck by tracking it. "We even helped him drag it out of the woods," she said proudly. Leanne smiled and said, "I helped too." A fitting reply from my future hunters.

A SPECIAL PLACE

by Roger C. Chriscoe, Asheboro, NC

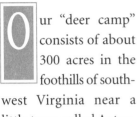

Our "deer camp" consists of about 300 acres in the foothills of southwest Virginia near a little town called Axton. The cabin is five years old and was built with logs cut from the mountains.

I decided a few years back that if I could relate with my two sons (Chad, 13 and Tyler, 9), we also needed a special place to relate to. I wanted my wife to be part of this as well. We've also introduced the boys' friends to the great outdoors, and hopefully will be able to keep them out of trouble and away from drugs.

I've come to realize that a real "trophy" is something you can share with good friends and a great family.

"I don't care how exciting your hunting trip to Exoor III was, you're not hanging that in here!"

THE YOUNGEST GAME CHEF

*by NAHC Member Bruce
Knight, Minneapolis, MN*

One fine day during last year's grouse season, I was walking down the gravel road toward my lake cabin in northern Wisconsin. As I passed the cabin of my neighbors, Chris and Wanda Headley, I noticed a trail of smoke coming out of the side door. It looked as though no one was home at the time because there were no cars or trucks in the driveway, so I figured I had better investigate what looked like a bad situation.

Opening the side door that led straight into the kitchen, I felt like I was walking into a scene from Dante's Inferno (or Emily Post's worst nightmare). Cracked eggshells dripped from the table. An explosion of flour dusted the floor, the countertops and the refrigerator door. And presiding over a smoking kettle on the stove was 8-year-old Chad Headley.

He looked up from the kettle, which was overflowing with boiling butter. "Hi, Bruce," he chirped, reaching into the kettle with tongs and extracting something that looked like a cross between a headless Barbie doll and a Kingsford briquet. "Want some?"

Now, Chris and Wanda have tried to raise Chad properly. When they gave him his dad's old .22 and taught him to shoot, they also made it clear that the house rule was, "If you shoot it, you eat it." Unfortunately, the rifle didn't come with a copy of *The Joy of Cooking*. So after his morning squirrel hunt with his dad, when Chad decided to make breaded fried squirrel for lunch, his cooking technique was not exactly that of a four-star chef.

I still chuckle when I remember the look of horror on Wanda's face when she came home a few minutes later. She wasn't sure who she should call first: the Bass Lake Fire Department, the local division of Merry Maids, or an adoption agency!

In addition to hunting, Chad also enjoys fishing with his dad and other friends. I snapped a photo of him during a recent Canada ice-fishing trip, with a pile of nice fish we'd caught. Chad was pretty excited about cooking that big northern in the photo. "Bruce," he said, "let's have breaded fish for dinner! I know how to fix it!" Well, maybe with a little help …

My wife Nancy and I always enjoy the time we spend with the Headleys when we go to our place in Wisconsin; in fact, they've invited us to dinner tonight at their cabin. Uh oh, I better go have a snack before dinner; I think I just saw Chad out back with the .22, chasing a flock of grackles! 🖎

Tips for Tastier Game

Here are some things that help ensure top-quality game dinners.

• If you're hunting in very hot weather, speed is of the essence in field dressing. For big game, get that body cavity opened and emptied as quickly as possible, then move the game into shade. For birds and small game, field-dress and fill the cavity with *dry* grass or straw; keep a cooler in the car for the trip home.

• When you package venison for the freezer, package in larger cuts rather than pre-cutting individual steaks, which lose more moisture to freezer burn. Cut the steaks after you thaw the meat, right before cooking.

• Plastic freezer-weight bags are great for ground meat. Pack them tightly, then dip them almost to the top in a sink filled with cold water. This forces out air, which causes freezer burn.

• Freeze small game or cut-up birds in water to prevent freezer burn. Well-washed waxed dairy cartons work well, as do freezer-weight plastic bags or plastic food-storage containers.

A TEEN'S FIRST HUNT

by Lesli Donovan (age 14),
Daughter of Life Member
Patrick Donovan, Hazen, ND

It all started when we talked about getting a deer application. I was so excited. On the day the license came I was so thrilled.

A few weeks later it was time to go. Every sound I heard I had to see what it was. One deer got close enough to shoot. My dad said, "Take your time, and shoot right behind the leg." I hit the deer in the left front leg. It ran a little ways and stopped. I shot again and

the deer stopped moving. I was happy and sad all at the same time. I took my first deer on September 20, 1997.

My dad helped me gut it out. When we got home, some of my dad's friends came to see my deer. The tenderloins tasted good on the grill. The sausage and jerky didn't taste half bad either.

I like to hunt because my dad hunts. It is fun, because you are always waiting for some animal to come out so you can shoot. I also hunt turkeys and waterfowl and shoot bows and arrows.

Venison with Roasted Garlic Cloves

      Venison saddle roast, 4 to 6 pounds
- 1 bottle (750 ml) dry red wine
- 1 cup virgin olive oil, plus additional for browning
- 2 bay leaves
- 2 tablespoons chopped parsley
- 2 teaspoons crumbled dried rosemary leaves
- 1 teaspoon crumbled dried savory
- 2 teaspoons cracked black pepper
- 1 teaspoon salt
- 8–10 whole garlic heads
- 6 strips smoked bacon

Place roast in large food-storage bag or very large bowl. Combine wine, 1 cup olive oil, bay leaves, parsley, rosemary, savory, black pepper and salt. Pour over meat. Seal bag or cover bowl and refrigerate two days, turning meat several times each day in the marinade.

Heat oven to 450°F. Remove meat from the marinade and pat dry; strain marinade and reserve in refrigerator. Heat 2 tablespoons olive oil in stovetop-safe roasting pan over medium-high heat; add roast and brown on all sides, adding additional oil if needed.

While the roast is browning, wash the garlic heads, discarding any skins that are very loose. Cut the tops off the garlic heads, exposing the individual cloves; trim bottom if necessary, leaving cloves attached at the base. Dip the cut surface of the garlic heads in olive oil and arrange around the browned roast. Cover roasting pan tightly and bake 30 minutes. Arrange bacon strips on top of roast. Reduce heat to 375°F and bake 30 minutes longer. Check internal temperature of the roast with a meat thermometer; meat should be 140°F to 150°F. Continue cooking a bit longer if necessary, but do not overcook.

To serve, lift meat and garlic out of roaster; keep warm. Add strained marinade to drippings in roaster and heat to boiling. Serve in gravy boat with sliced roast; each person squeezes the cooked garlic cloves out of the skins to garnish their meat.

from NAHC member David W. Dowdy, Crab Orchard, WV

Eric Nisch

Hometown:	Rensselaerville, NY
Species:	Eastern Wild Turkey
Weapon:	NEF 10 gauge, Remington 3½" #4 Premium Turkey Loads
Hunting state:	New York

"The night previous to the hunt we heard the turkey gobble while we were cutting wood with a chain saw. Before dawn I set up where I thought he was. He dropped out of a tree not 50 yards from me and came right to my decoys."

"Geez, Tom… 'catch-and-release' is something you do in fishing—not in bear hunting!"

THE SHOOTING FAMILY

by Bob Allen, North American Hunter *columnist*

For the past 100 years or so, the shooting sports have been considered pretty much a man's game. A boy became an adult when he could shoulder a shotgun and make a bird dog mind. Everything about the sport, from recoil to rattlesnakes, was part of being one of the guys.

I'll be the first to admit that there are many who would like to keep it an all-male domain, but there are many more who would love to get the gals and kids involved. The struggle is that the shooting sports are primarily male-geared in terms of attitudes and equipment.

Many women and kids have a terrible first experience, and if they do, who can blame them when they won't go back a second time? So it goes as everyone talks about the demise of the family and the lack of quality time. In reality, shotgun sports can be the perfect family activity.

What better way to teach a youngster responsibility, values, conservation and good sportsmanship? And where else can you break things and still impress your wife? The key to having a good experience is being prepared, so plan the first introduction carefully.

Don't expect a young boy or girl or even your wife to be able to hit targets with a shotgun designed for the average 175-pound American male. More than likely the stock will be too long, the gun will balance too far forward and the recoil will make them quit before the first box of shells is finished. Proper gun fit is imperative to hitting objects in the air.

Many companies are now producing youth and ladies' model shotguns designed for shooters with smaller frames. They're a good investment, especially if there are a couple of young shooters in the family and the gun can be shared or passed down. The other alternative is to buy an extra stock and cut it down to the proper

©ANDERSON

A cow pasture is a great place to introduce the family to wingshooting. Pick a day when you won't be rushed or distracted by other commitments. It will also help if the weather is cool. Hot days can lead to frustration and compound problems. Pack a picnic, a cooler full of soda pop and a hand thrower and head for the country.

Keep a positive attitude and position the shooter where he or she can shoot at straight-away targets. These are the easiest to break and there is nothing like those puffs of black smoke to bolster a shooter's confidence. Gradually work into some angle and crossing shots while stressing those two ever-important basics—keep both eyes open and keep that barrel moving. Don't forget the ear and eye protection.

After the new shooter has learned the basics of gun safety and shot some hand-thrown birds, it's time for sporting clays. Courses can be found within easy driving distances of most cities, and a day on the course is the perfect family outing. Tell the

length. The original can be saved until the shooter grows into it.

The right stock will not only help with shooting, it will cut down on the felt recoil. Recoil reduction can be taken several steps further with barrel porting and in-stock devices. Gas-operated autoloaders kick less by design and make great first guns. Shells can be loaded one at a time and the magazine can be plugged to permit only one shell in the chamber while hunting. If budget permits, a good-quality over and under also makes a good choice, but don't let the expense of a new shotgun stand in the way of introducing new shooters to the sport.

manager ahead of time that you'll be bringing your family with you. If he knows beforehand, he can start you out at a time and position where you won't feel pressured to hurry through the stations. Many courses can also provide low-cost entry-level instruction; sometimes it's even free for the asking.

Sporting clays are great for novice shooters because not even the experts break every bird. In fact, the first time through, don't even keep score, just enjoy the time and the outdoors.

Contrary to popular belief, sporting clays circles are not dominated by snobbish know-it-alls in tweed jackets. In fact, even the best shooters dress pretty casual on practice days. Though many accessories are available, they can be added as a shooter progresses through the sport. Shoot every bird with an improved choke the first time through and worry about the fine tuning later on down the road.

Most of all, have fun. Laugh and joke with your wife and kids, and remember the first time *you* tossed a tin can in the air. 🖎

Mary Barthel

Hometown:	Rayville, LA
Species:	Rio Grande Wild Turkey
Weapon:	20-gauge Remington
Hunting state:	Texas
Guide:	My Mother

"My mother called the turkey up for me and I shot it. It was the most happiest day of mine and her life."

"Fred, I think you better give that friction call a little rest."

MAKING A DIFFERENCE

by Tom Carpenter,
NAHC Staff Member

Some kids are different.

Take kids who grow up around hunting. My first memories are not of a certain birthday present, or a visit to somewhere special, or any of a dozen other run-of-the-mill things that could have stuck with me after so long.

Rather, I recall meeting my father in the garage whenever he returned from some golden October day of squirrel hunting. I'd unload his game vest, carefully laying out the squirrels from within and enjoying the smells of fur, and of oak and hickory forests, that they brought me.

Little things like that made me a hunter, and changed my life—I think for the better. Most of us could agree: Hunting has made us better people and added dimensions of the outdoors, wildness, adventure, and yes, even some compassion, to life.

But what about the kids of today? Are they going to have the opportunity to be different?

You know the statistics: We're not recruiting hunters into the fold fast enough to replace those of us who are dropping out due to age or indifference or because it has just become too much work.

Fewer hunters in the field won't mean better hunting for those left. It will only mean we're closer to losing this most glorious of rights and privileges: hunting, just being there in good country with people you love and the game you love too in a hunter's sort of way.

So make a difference.

If you have your own kids, boys *or* girls, take the time to take them hunting. No, it's not easy in today's urbanized and suburbanized world. But think of the difference it has made for you and the benefits the kids will get over watching TV, staring at a computer screen, going to the mall or just hanging out. The work is worth it, and time is the best thing you can ever give a kid.

If your kids are grown and gone, or if you don't have any, find one to introduce to hunting. Maybe it's the son or daugh-

ter of a neighbor, a co-worker, someone from your place of worship—there is no shortage of children (many from one-parent homes) who would never otherwise get the chance to hunt.

Then be smart about hooking them. Start slow. Talk a lot about the hunting—pheasants or small game or maybe even deer—that you want to start them out on. Tell your stories—they will love it and you'll find yourself getting to spin your old yarns again and again to a captive and interested audience.

Go to the target range with your bows, rifles or shotguns; make sure the new hunter is outfitted properly with a firearm or archery gear they can handle, and clothes, boots and other gear that makes sense.

Feed them magazines and books with lots of pictures. Answer questions, ask them for questions. Remember—this is a whole new world for them and you are the expert. Every question is good, and all these things—tracks, sign, game habits and habitat, hunting strategies, shot placement, field dressing—are fascinating to your new hunter. Chances are, you'll get the spark to hone up some more on your own knowledge as well.

That's it.

As a hunter, you have a gift: knowledge of a grand and storied outdoor sport that needs all the support it can get. And as a hunter, you also have power: the power to change a life (or lives) by introducing young people to the outdoors and hunting.

Give kids the chance to be different. Teach them how to love the outdoors, how to hunt. You'll make a big difference in their lives, and probably even in your own. ☞

• IT'S A SMALL WORLD •
Rabbits and squirrels and hares, oh my!

1. Which of the following statements about cottontails are true? (mark all that apply)
   a. When alarmed, cottontails bolt in a straight line to escape.
   b. Although cottontails don't spend much time underground, a pursued rabbit may take cover in a woodchuck burrow.
   c. Rabbits have teeth on the upper jaw only.

2. In a prime squirrel woods, how many gray squirrels are likely to be in each acre?
   a. 4 or more squirrels per acre
   b. 3 squirrels per acre
   c. 1 squirrel per acre

3. Which of the following are characteristic of raccoon behavior? (mark all that apply)
   a. They will run around a pond rather than enter the water because they are poor swimmers.
   b. They can run as fast as 15 mph.
   c. When chased by dogs, a raccoon may crawl into a hole in the ground.

4. Which of the following statements about rabbits and hares are true? (mark all that apply)
   a. Rabbits are born hairless and blind, while hares are born with fur and open eyes.
   b. Rabbits are much more prolific than hares, producing several litters per year compared to the hare's one litter.
   c. Hares will run to avoid predators, while rabbits are more likely to hide.

5. *True or false:* If you see a squirrel with black fur, it is actually an Eastern gray squirrel.

Answers are on page 148.

Small Game Hunting Tips And Tidbits

- Cottontails often hide in large brushpiles because they are safe from hawks in the tangle. To get them out, beat the brush pile with a stick, or have a partner climb on top and shake the pile while you stand ready for a shot.

- Squirrels can be called by tapping two small stones together. Or, place two quarters in your fingertips and click them together. In both cases, a squirrel will come out to investigate what all the "scolding" is about.

- To catch a squirrel at its game of hiding on the opposite side of a tree, tie a string to a bush and move to the opposite side. Pull the string to shake the bush, and get ready for action. Some hunters tie a piece of red felt to the bush along with the string to provide more distraction for the squirrel.

- Wait for a fresh snowfall, then strap on a pair of snowshoes to track snowshoe hares. Longer snowshoes provide more lift; snowshoes with pointed tips that curve upward are easier to maneuver in tangled forests.

"…I thought Frank had a hip replacement…"

Matt Hill

Matt Hill
NAHC Member

James Pace
Friend

Hometown:	Nashville, TN
Species:	Mallard Ducks
Weapon:	Remington 870 Express 12-gauge #2 Winchester Super "X" Steel Shot
Hunting state:	Arkansas

"It was a great hunt! The birds never stopped coming, we couldn't have asked for anything more."

Members Write About HUNTING CAMP

WARMEST PLACE I KNOW
by Tom Kleist, Eagle Lake, MN

A thin layer of plastic, opaque now with duct tape patching, is supported by a 2x2 framework of begged and borrowed lumber. Though not made with the most efficient building materials, the shack is the warmest place I know.

Heat, and an orange glow, is cast by a rust-thin barrel stove. The strong, hazy scent of wood smoke is overpowered, however, by the smell of split pine, wet wool and two-bit cigars.

Twelve warm bodies—some visitors, some who call this place home temporarily—cram into this one-room shack. Experiences are exchanged, stories are told, and there is laughter. Young ears

listen, trying to hear four separate speakers. I listen too and wait patiently to hear familiar stories, those told annually, to see how much has changed from the last time it was told.

As supper draws near I walk our company to the door. Outside, my nose welcomes the cold, clean air. A zillion tiny stars and a sliver of moon light the sky. I say goodbye and head back to the shack. An old red lantern, lashed to a sapling tripod, throws a welcome yellow light. Returning from each day's hunt, night chasing me home, the light beckons, signalling home.

As the door slams behind me, I remove fogged lenses and smile. Deer camp is the companionship; I am glad I am here. I join the laughter and am warmed spiritually too.

CHARLIE'S DEER

by John Sloan, North American Hunter *contributing writer*

They came just as the sun had melted the frost enough to turn it to water, which then dripped from the multicolored leaves. They materialized from the pine grove and slid slowly toward him, their movement accented by occasional head jerks and tail twitches.

Two mature does out for a morning walk.

The wind was perfect, and the big tree trunk gave him ideal cover. He watched them as they stared intently at nothing, licking their noses and swiveling their ears. No bumbling youngsters, these two does.

The scarred, old bow rested across his knees. Sunlight glinted off the shining, razor-sharp broadhead. He couldn't really say why he chose the bow over the Remington today. It just felt right.

The first deer paused at the brilliantly colored maple tree. The second was a half-dozen steps behind. It was only 20 yards, and the doe was broadside. He could make the shot easily. He had a doe tag and was not against shooting a doe and letting a small buck walk. But the deer were headed for Charlie, and Charlie had only this one day to hunt before returning to college. These were Charlie's deer. He never thought otherwise.

The does moved on, their herky-jerky ambulation taking them directly down the draw and straight toward Charlie. Charlie's favorite stand was in an oak tree, screened from the travel pattern by a beech. It was not the best stand on the lease, but Charlie liked it because the creek ran shallow there and giggled as it turned over rocks and gravel. It was a pretty place, just a bit too open for the bigger bucks. The man knew that Charlie didn't care.

This was Charlie's third year of deer hunting with him. So far, Charlie had not fired a shot. The .243 Win., except for practice rounds and annual trip to the range, didn't see much action.

He suddenly became aware that he was holding his breath, listening for the spat of the rifle. He regulated his breathing and strained his ears. Admittedly, his hearing wasn't what it once was. He noticed that a lot of deer got pretty close to him before he heard them walking. But he would hear the rifle. Charlie was only 200 yards up the draw.

A blue jay did a balancing act on a slender branch above his head, and a pair of acorns plopped by his leg. He thumbed his hat back a little, hoping to improve his hearing. Fifteen minutes took an hour to pass.

Nothing.

He slowly rolled to his feet, taking time to allow his back muscles to unkink and to make sure both knees had locked before he took a step. Making himself walk slowly, he moved up the draw, unconsciously taking the same route that the does had traveled toward Charlie.

Charlie was watching him as he moved through the trees. Finally he looked up, silently questioning. Charlie shrugged, her blond hair shining. She held up two fingers and grinned.

"Well, Charlie," he said, "couldn't shoot again, huh?"

"Oh, Dad, I just come to hunt and watch, you know that. I just like being out in the woods with you. Maybe I'll shoot a deer some day. Maybe not. I'm just hunting, and I told you, my name is Charlotte."

He turned and looked into the woods, pretending to hear something suddenly. As he adjusted his hat and hitched his pants, he wiped the corner of his eye.

"Sure a pretty morning, huh? Ready for some breakfast?"

"Yeah, and you bet I'm ready for breakfast. I want three eggs and bacon and toast and maybe some hash browns. Dad, I'll be home again next weekend. We can come again and maybe I'll shoot next time."

"Girl, you don't have to shoot to please me. Just seeing you sitting there in that tree is a pleasure, knowing you saw what I saw and enjoyed the morning."

The sun had topped the ridge, and the air warmed as the two hunters walked the old logging road that wound through the oaks. It had been a great day in the deer woods, and the two hunters thought about the next time they could watch a sunrise at this very special place.

Woodcock Hot Legs

Wily little woodcocks are not only a joy to hunt, they are a gourmet's delight on the table as well. Most hunters take the breast meat and discard everything else, including the legs. Granted, there isn't a whole lot of meat on those spindly legs, but what's there is delicious white meat. One woodcock won't do. I save them up until I have maybe two dozen legs, depending on how many people I want to serve.

- ½ teaspoon black pepper
- ½ cup barbecue sauce
- Tabasco sauce to taste
- 1 tablespoon butter
- 24 or more woodcock legs, skinned
- Prepared blue cheese dressing

In small bowl, blend barbecue sauce, pepper and Tabasco sauce. Melt butter in large skillet over medium heat, then add woodcock legs and cook until nicely browned, 3 to 4 minutes. Add the barbecue sauce mixture; reduce heat and simmer for about 10 minutes. Place blue cheese dressing in a small bowl on a larger plate; arrange legs around bowl of dressing and serve while legs are hot.

Artwork and recipe by NAHC member Ed Sutton, Delton, MI

TAKE IT FROM ME

by NAHC Member Aaron Alsheimer, Bath, NY

When you stop and think about everything that has gone on in the world of sports during the last few years, one thing stands out more than any other—the dominance of youth. Okay, I know. John Elway won two Superbowls in the last years of his career and Dale Earhardt finally made it into the victory lane at Daytona. But throw those two out of the picture and look at what's left. Kevin Garnett and Kobe Bryant played in the NBA All-Star Game shortly after their 20th birthdays. Tiger Woods left college and almost immediately established himself as one of the best golfers in the world, and 15-year-old Tara Lipinsky became the youngest gold medalist in Olympic history. Obviously, young people are establishing their presence in sports like never before.

You can see this trend in just about every major American sport except for one—hunting. Instead of increasing, the number of young people who take an active interest in hunting, and more specifically bowhunting, has dropped considerably from where it once was. And that's sad, because bowhunting is much more than a "sport." And, at least to me, it has deeper meaning than other sports and hobbies I enjoy.

A lot of the drop-off in interest is due to the fact that most kids just don't know what they're missing. You might be at the point where you are wondering whether you should get into bowhunting but don't know if it's worth it. Before you make up your mind, let me tell you what bowhunting has meant to me. Then maybe you'll have a better idea of why it's too fun to pass up.

My background pretty much guaranteed that I would at least try bowhunting. My dad is an outdoor writer, and he made sure to introduce me to hunting at an early age. When I was eight or nine, my parents gave me my first bow for Christmas. It was fairly simple by today's standards, but it gave me plenty of fun-filled hours of target practice in the basement of my family's home.

In October of 1991, I turned 14 and was able to hunt deer with a bow for the first time. My experiences from the last seven bowhunting seasons have taught me to appreciate both the beauty of nature and the challenge of pursuing whitetails.

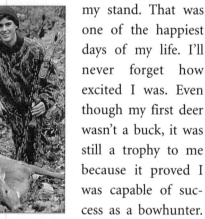

I'll admit that there are some times when it seems like there isn't a deer left on the face of the earth, but the moment that one finally appears in the distance makes all the waiting worthwhile. Few experiences can match it. Even if the chance for a shot never develops, the opportunity to have an up-close look at such an incredible animal is something you'll never forget.

One day I'll never forget was the day I took my first deer with a bow and arrow. It was the first Saturday of my third season. Shortly after I got into my stand in mid-afternoon, two does appeared in front of me and started moving in my direction. Finally, after what seemed like an eternity, one of them stepped into an opening to my left, and I released the arrow. The shot was on target, and the doe went down just a short distance from my stand. That was one of the happiest days of my life. I'll never forget how excited I was. Even though my first deer wasn't a buck, it was still a trophy to me because it proved I was capable of success as a bowhunter.

Since that first taste of success, I've spent many hours in the deer woods. Through it all, using a bow has become my favorite way to hunt.

There are several reasons why I like bowhunting so much. First, it allows me to get a close-up look at nature. I've been able to witness some unbelievable white-tailed deer behavior during bow seasons over the years. Even when I haven't seen deer, I've enjoyed watching gray squirrels scurry around collecting acorns or raccoons wandering through the woods. The outdoors is great, but you can't really appreciate it until you experience it first-hand. You can't get it from a computer.

I also enjoy bowhunting because it presents a challenge that you don't find in other forms of hunting. It forces you to hold off on shooting until the animal is within close range.

Finally, the time of year we have our bow season where I live in New York is beautiful. The autumn colors are at their peak, and the weather hasn't yet taken an ugly turn. Gun season is still to come, so the deer are relatively undisturbed. It's just a great time to be in the woods.

The memories I have of my experiences hunting deer with a bow are really special to me. Tell your mom or dad that you'd like to try it. By the time archery season comes around, you'll be ready to step into the deer woods and experience what bowhunting is all about.

Take it from me—you'll be glad you tried this exciting pursuit.

Gene White

Hometown: Flagler Beach, FL
Species: American Elk
Weapon: PSE–Thunderhead
Hunting state: Jicarilla Apache Tribe, New Mexico
Guide: Eugene Chavez

"When the bull turned his head and I saw the 51" spread I got shook, and my first shot went between the bull's legs. It was so far off he didn't spook and I was able to get in position for a 45-yard shot as he was getting back to his cows."

"I didn't become a trophy buck falling for something like that!"

William Bos

Hometown:	Kalamazoo, MI
Species:	Stone Sheep (B&C 146%)
Weapon:	Remington 7mm, Hornady Custom 154 gr.
Hunting state:	British Columbia (Canada)
Guide:	Jennings River Outfitters

Learning To Estimate Range

One of the hardest chores for beginning hunters is learning to estimate shooting range. For long-range shots at big game, it's important to estimate distance accurately to calculate bullet drop; for birds and small game, it's vital to know when the target is "in range" to avoid shots that merely cripple. Here are some pointers to help novice and experienced hunters alike.

Use your duplex scope as a rangefinder

Antelope is 400 yards away

Greater than 400 yards

Learn the distance covered by the thin wires in the center of your duplex scope at a specific power. For example, at 8x power, the distance might be 40 inches at 400 yards. Next, determine the body length of the game you're after. Pronghorn, for example, are about 40 inches from chest to rump, so at 400 yards, the pronghorn's body would just fit between the thick blades at 8x power. This information will help you adjust your aim point. If the pronghorn is much smaller than the thin wire area, you know that it is more than 400 yards away. Learn this information for the specific scope you'll be using; if you switch to another scope, don't assume the distances are the same.

Pace off around your deer stand or turkey blind

First, determine how many steps you must take to travel five yards. Then, before you get on stand or set up in a spot for turkeys, pace off distances to a specific tree, rock or other identifiable object. When game appears, you'll know how far away it is. For deer hunting, it's also helpful to visualize distances such as 50 yards, 100 yards and so on. Go to a shooting range and visualize what a deer would look like at the 50-yard range, for example.

Place a confidence decoy at 35 yards

When you set up duck or goose decoys, place a confidence decoy (or other distinctive decoy) 35 yards from your shooting position. By drawing an imaginary arc from that decoy, you can determine when birds are within safe shooting range.

CONTINUING TRADITIONS
by Life Member Frank Bolyard,
Flemington, WV

I came from a family of seven boys and one girl. As we began to move away from home, we realized we needed a place to gather in the fall to continue our hunting traditions. My wife, Shawn, and I decided to build a cabin on the back side of my father's 250-acre farm.

I went to the library and found a book explaining the Scandinavian method of building a log cabin. As Shawn peeled the bark from the poplar logs with a draw knife, I would trim and fit them together. Our daughter Misty and son Luke also helped; some of my brothers helped with the roof and floor, making it a family project.

Today the cabin is used by family and friends alike. We are building memories every year—from Luke's first deer, to the big 10-point buck my brother Doug shot behind the big rock stand, to the time I put salt in the koolade instead of sugar, to the time my brother Brian brought his father-in-law up to hunt (if anyone ever insists on sleeping in the truck because they snore, don't try to convince them otherwise). We remember all these stories and tell them over and over, year after year, to the delight of young and old alike. That is how we are continuing our hunting traditions.

Scott Zwick

Hometown:	Sauk Rapids, MN
Species:	Canada geese
Weapon:	12-gauge Winchester 1300, Federal Tungsten-Iron
Hunting state:	Minnesota

"I was hunting with my father. We were on our own private land. When a flock of about 20 geese came in, we both shot at the same one and it fell. We then both took another shot and two more fell; another fell about 200 yards away from a stray pellet. All together we shot four geese on my first goose hunt."

BEYOND BEGINNER'S LUCK

by Michael Faw,
NAHC staff member

"Yeah, I see them!" 16-year-old Chris Koffel excitedly whispered as he slid the muzzleloader's thick barrel out through the small opening of our blind and tucked the butt of the smokepole to his shoulder. We were huddled in a ground blind in the South Texas brush country on a crisp January morning. The first rays of daylight began to brighten the region around us, revealing a small herd of 10 deer feeding and milling about near our blind. A great moment in modern hunting history as Texas' new muzzleloader antlerless deer season had officially arrived.

Chris nervously pulled the hammer back, peered through the scope to select a deer and steadied for the shot. At the pull of the trigger, the cap exploded but the louder blast we expected to follow never occurred. Fortunately, the deer in front of our blind never heard the noise and continued to feed and mill about.

A few minutes later, however, all the deer's heads snapped to attention, and they dashed off through the brush and away from our location. Something to our right had spooked them. I could see the disheartened look sweep across Chris' face as he glanced over his shoulder at me.

The enthusiasm and nervous hunter's quiver of excitement returned in Chris shortly after, though, as a lone white-tailed deer walked across the horizon and came on a course for our blind. This time when young Chris shouldered the muzzleloader and pulled the trigger, the lead flew true over 10 yards, and the result was more hunting history. The deer made a short dash and collapsed as we watched.

"All right, I got it!" Chris exclaimed. I could tell by his excited voice and record-book grin that the ranks of the hunting community had just increased by one. Amazingly, I saw the same pride of accomplishment and the thrill of becoming a successful hunter sweep across the face of a couple more young hunters that day and the next as the hunting community grew.

Chris Koffel's blackpowder deer

Even more amazing was that a mere 24 hours earlier these new young hunters had never hunted and many had never fired—or even held—a gun.

The trip to the range a few hours after their arrival introduced most of the soon-to-be hunters to muzzleloading rifles. There they learned sight-in techniques and how to load and clean the long guns. In addition, they attended classes about hunter safety and wildlife conservation.

What a difference a day makes under the right conditions. Thanks to the efforts of companies like Swarovski Optik, White Shooting Systems, Dixie Gun Works, Bushland Camouflage, Thompson/Center Arms, Blount, Buck Knives, Butler Creek and numerous other blackpowder

hunting equipment manufacturers, important transformations occurred in the lives of 20 young hunters. Significant transformations also took place in the lives of their guides and mentors, myself included, through our participation. We helped our charges along in grand fashion as they joined the ranks of accomplished hunters.

"All of the kids proved it," stated Swarovski Optik's President Jim Morey. "They had a safe, positive experience with blackpowder firearms and had fun at the same time." Jim was talking just as excitedly as the youths. His dream had come true along with those of the apprentice hunters on this hunt. As he introduces youngsters from nonhunting families to hunting, Jim's dream could change the face of hunting.

These new hunters can then influence their friends, and in turn, introduce future generations to the thrill of hunting. This event was proof that kids can handle guns safely if adults take the time to show them the correct way.

Jim Morey's idea culminated in a four-day trip to the Y.O. and Ponda Rosa Ranches for the young hunters. There they joined a cadre of experienced hunters who made the transition into the ranks of a successful hunter a smooth one.

The apprentice hunters arrived at the Y.O. Ranch from all regions of Texas as the sponsors and guides worked behind the scenes to prepare equipment and assemble support kits for them. Each novice hunter traveled as the guest of a sponsor, and each sponsor provided background details and a physical assessment of the hunter. This information was taken into consideration for matching the hunter with his firearm, equipment, mentor and hunting location. Safety and opportunity for success were given top priority in planning for the hunt.

The night before the hunt, beside a spectacular bonfire, each apprentice hunter and mentor were paired up and given a few minutes to finalize last-minute plans and get acquainted. Chris and I first met in the shadows by the flickering fire and shared our enthusiasm for the hunt we'd share on the next day. Chris's excitement and his attention to every detail made my job easy.

The next day, Chris's introduction to hunting didn't stop after the smoke from the shot vanished. He field-dressed his deer as I coached and gave technical pointers. Even placing the tag on the carcass brought on a discussion about game laws and game management. Obviously, details like this are best learned first-hand in the field and not in some distant classroom. Hunting teaches a valuable lesson.

More important than the hunt was the responsibility the new hunters shouldered after they were successful. The new hunters skinned and quartered their own deer. Each hunter later returned home with a cooler of venison to share with family and friends. Many kept their deer hides to make rugs as a reminder of the experience.

The group of new hunters included inner-city kids who came from diverse backgrounds, some of which were less than ideal conditions to grow up in. They handled the responsibility of firearms safety and camp etiquette at a level many adults could learn from.

Near the end of the trip, huntmaster Denny Vasquez from Houston commented, "Without the support of organizations like the North American Hunting Club, we would have been unable to provide this experience for the youths who participated." Vasquez plans to build this into a national program that will get hunters mentoring more apprentice hunters all across America. 🐾

"President, phooey! Take me to your whitetails!"

DEER CAMP GENERATIONS
by various NAHC members

"The name of our camp is Summit West Hunting Lodge; it's located near Bergton, Virginia. Opening week of rifle season is a big event at

our cabin, with my extended family of brothers-in-law, all of our sons and some daughters as well as a few special friends. Some of our most enjoyable and important memories are the times we share with our sons and daughters in the hunting camp. The kids are all ears and simply devour the stories told at camp. We all wish they were that attentive in school!"
–Sam Fullerton, Manassas, VA

"In 1976 a few friends and I decided to lease a few acres from the state of Minnesota, and we got a cutting permit. Not knowing what we were doing, we went ahead and constructed our cabin out of mostly logs. More than twenty years later, it still stands. Most of the original owners are still members. Now we have a new generation of hunters—our kids who really enjoy and appreciate what we have here. I must say, the main guy who pushed us to build this was my dad. He hunted every year, but now he just visits, eats our food and drinks our beer. My hat's off to him."
–Robert A. Almquist, Gilbert, MN

"Poker Flats is what a deer camp is all about. It's steeped in family tradition— some very old, some created just last year. We moved a log cabin that my grandpa built to our present site and have been adding on ever since. Our kids have gone from babes in arms to college grads, spending time at the shack; and pretty soon, I suspect another generation will be coming along. Poker Flats is located in the town of Chelsea in Taylor County, Wisconsin."
–Dave Zuleger, Medford, WI

"When I was finally old enough to go to 'hunting camp' it was to the one my Dad and his oldest brother, Walt, had built on the Stannard Mountain in upstate Vermont. Later my dad, two older brothers and I acquired 13 acres known as the 'Triangle Piece' from my uncle and with the help of a few friends, put up a 24' x 24' stick-frame building with a loft. My brothers' sons are now old enough to go to 'hunting camp' and carry on the traditions and to hike those hardwood ridges in search of the elusive whitetail buck. Dad turned 81 years young last year, and

although he doesn't hike to the top of the mountain anymore, he still goes to camp and with the help of his 4-wheeler, can still get out to his deer stand. I don't get home as often as I'd like, but when I do, camp is the first place I go. There's always a strong feeling of coming home when I walk through the door." *–Life Member Jeffrey L. Scott, Victor, ID*

MUSINGS OF AN ANTELOPE JUNKIE

by NAHC Member Teresa Marrone, Minneapolis, MN

I'll admit it: Antelope hunting is my favorite. From the Western scenery (so very different from that in my home state of Minnesota) to the warm, friendly ranchers and folks I encounter in the small towns to the delicious meat I bring home for the freezer, "goat hunting" is hard to beat.

I wasn't born to a hunting family, though, so I came to the sport as an adult. I remember my first Wyoming antelope hunt. At the age of 31, I was the only "girl" with a bunch of guys. Our plan was to camp out in the rancher's sheep-breeding pens; luckily, the sheep were out on the range at that time of year, so we had the area—such as it was—to ourselves. The guys were going to bunk on cots inside one of the pens; another pen was turned into a service-able kitchen. Since these guys were to me more on the order of work acquaintances than bosom buddies, I decided I wanted a bit of privacy, so I brought along a small rented tent, which I pitched at the end of the sheep run. There wasn't much for modern conveniences: An out-house and a hose with cold run-ning water was about it. But I was game, and determined to have a good time.

On opening morning, I was dropped off about two miles from camp and set off to do a little stalking. I glassed a distant valley and saw a big herd, so I decided to go for it. I figured that once I got close, I would crawl on my belly, military-style, until I was within range. I was so pumped up that I didn't even feel all those cactus spines jam-ming into my forearms, legs, knees and elbows. The antelope definitely saw me, but I don't think they knew what to do about this "thing" that was creeping, crab-like, toward them; I was probably the first human dumb enough to crawl through 600 yards of cactus thicket to get at them.

I finally got to a point where I thought I could make the shot, and steadied the .280 Remington on my pack. The big buck was presenting a nice broadside shot, and I got him down. It was only as I was rolling up my sleeves to begin field-dressing that I noticed my arms looked like a hedge-pig from all the cactus spines!

That night, a good meal and a little nip of Mr. Beam helped me forget my pincushion anatomy; I slept like a rock. The next morning, I awoke to the sound of a very heavy rain. I began to peel back the sleeping bag, and noticed that it was ... wet. *Really* wet. That rental tent was, shall we say, not exactly new, and nowhere near waterproof. It was leaking heavily from the bottom.

Now, if you're following this story, you'll recall that my little nylon shack was pitched in the middle of a sheep run. Well, let's just say that the rancher had not taken the Hoover out there to clean up the grounds before we came; so my sleeping bag was now lying in a sea of *liquefied sheep droppings!* Holy sheep ... I mean cow. The foot of the bag, where it had slipped off the air mattress, was completely saturated, as were the sides and the half-opened flap at the top.

As I rolled out of this soggy mess, I was reminded of the cactus spines in various parts of my anatomy; since there wasn't a real bathroom facility, I hadn't attempted to do much about it the previous evening, merely pulling out the biggest offenders. I jammed my feet into my wet boots and headed for the mess pen.

The guys were sitting there looking glum because of the weather and were in no hurry to get out. So I decided to take off my stocking cap (which I had not taken off since the previous afternoon ... it's not like I was headed to any beauty pageant) and work at untangling my long hair, which I had jammed under the cap the day before. I immediately realized I had another problem. No way was a comb going through that tangled mess! One of the guys handed me his pocket comb, which clearly said UNBREAKABLE. Two swipes later, it snapped in two, half of it landing in a mud puddle. "Thanks," I mumbled as I handed the remaining half back to him. "I feel better now. Sorry about the comb." He ran his fingers through his thinning hair and admitted that it really didn't matter that much; half a comb was as good as a dozen, at that point.

This trip continued in similar fashion for about five days; that stocking cap never did come off again until we hit a motel in Rapid City, South Dakota, on the way back home. We picked the guy from the crew that looked the least disreputable, and made him go in to get rooms for us all. I snuck in the back door and the second I was in my room, stripped off all my clothes and stood under the shower for about half an hour, just letting the hot, soapy water run over me. I think I broke another comb getting through my hair that night.

That first trip set the pattern for many to come. I recall another trip a few years later, where I again tangled with those scrub cactus. I was hiking up a steep cow trail; as I paused for breath, I saw several 'lopes at the top of the hill. I figured, man, they've seen me! But I thought that if I sat down real quick-like, I might be able to get steady enough for a shot. Down I went, and planted my posterior—firmly—on a patch of low-growing cactus. I think I heard the goats snigger as they took off.

My hunting buddies came up to see what was happening, just as I was getting ready to drop my pants to pull out thorns (by this time, I'd learned to carry a tweezers). I politely invited them to "admire the view" in the other direction while I went about my business.

I could go on and on about the adventures I've had out West, chasing antelope. I've told my nonhunting friends about these trips, and they don't really understand how wild it can get out there. But they probably all remember this: For a month after that first trip, every time I put on a pair of nylons, I got a million runs in them from the cactus spines working their way out of my legs! It was actually a pleasant reminder—sitting in my plush suburban office and contemplating yet another pair of ruined stockings—of the wild and wooly West. 🐾

Hunter's Recipe File

Beer-Battered Gobbler

- 1 wild turkey, skin and bones removed
- 1 can (12 ounces) beer, approximately
- 1 cup all-purpose flour
- 2½ tablespoons seasoned salt
- 1½ tablespoons garlic salt
- Oil for deep frying

Cut turkey into strips approximately 2 inches long and 1 inch wide. Mix beer, flour, seasoned salt and garlic salt, adding enough beer to make a batter that is thin enough for dipping but not too thin. Dip turkey pieces in batter. Deep-fry until golden brown.

Note: This batter is also fantastic for any fish, as well as onion rings, dill pickle spears, pheasant and grouse.

from NAHC member Mike Groff, Mansfield, OH

"My guest tonight, turkey calling's Grand Champion…"

WHEN LIGHTNING STRIKES

by Steve Pennaz,
NAHC staff member

It was a cool, gray Sunday afternoon in late September when Chad Owens, 16, parked his Jeep in some woods surrounding his parents' farm near Cumberland, Wisconsin.

The bow season was open and Chad was hoping to arrow a whitetail. A light rain was falling as he walked quietly to his stand in a large pine tree. A deer trail passed almost directly beneath his perch and led to a cornfield a few hundred yards away. Many deer used the field as their evening feeding grounds, so Chad knew it was only a matter of time before one of them passed within range. He settled back to wait. Suddenly, without warning, a blot of lightning ripped out of the sky and struck the tree that Chad was in!

The stout pine weathered the blow, giving up strips of bark as the current streaked down it. But Chad wasn't so lucky. The lightning tore through his hat and continued down his body, burning flesh as it crossed his chest and ran the length of his leg. The current blew out the bottom of his boot before re-entering the tree to finish its journey to the ground. Chad, unconscious, fell to the ground—more than 15 feet below.

When Chad failed to return home at dusk, his parents weren't worried. They had seen the lightning and heard the tremendous clap of thunder, but never gave it a second thought. His father, Jon, had milking to do, and his mother, Ann, had a Concerned Parents meeting to attend in town. Besides, explained Ann, "Bowhunters never come home until after dark."

It wasn't until 8:00 p.m. that they started wondering if something was wrong. Jon knew exactly where Chad was hunting, so he drove to the spot to see if he could find him. The sight of Chad's Jeep confirmed that he was still in the woods, so Jon headed to Chad's stand, starting to worry if something was wrong.

His fears grew when he saw the scarred tree. Lightning had stripped bark down most of its length. The only unscathed spot was a six-foot section above the branch his son usually hunted from!

Looking around in a growing panic, Jon spotted Chad's hat. It had a hole burned through the middle of it! He knew then that Chad had been hit and rushed home to call his neighbors. A search party was quickly formed. Within 15 minutes more than 50 people showed up to offer their help. A handful of volunteers accompanied Jon as he headed back to the woods. The group spread out and began walking through the woods in a line, calling to Chad as they walked.

Fifteen minutes passed, then fifteen more. The searchers were beginning to wonder if they were walking in the wrong direction when they heard a faint answer. It was Chad!

Jon Owens was the first person to reach his son. "He didn't know where he was," said Jon, "or where he was going. He knew he was hurt but didn't know he had been struck by lightning. He thought he had dozed off and fallen out of his stand.

"His clothes were ripped to shreds. They were falling off because there was nothing left of them. The bottom of one of his boots was blown off. Even his underwear was ripped in two."

Chad spent the next five days in the hospital—two of them in intensive care. Doctors constantly monitored his heart as they treated his burns. He also had hurt his back, probably by hitting a tree root or rock.

Doctors speculate that the fall, or more precisely, the impact, may have saved Chad's life. They think the lightning stopped his heart and the impact of the fall may have jolted it enough to start it beating again.

Chad missed the remainder of the Cumberland High School football season, but he didn't miss much of the bow season. Two short weeks after being struck, he was back in his stand.

He didn't have to wait long before a fat Wisconsin whitetail ambled down the trail within range of his bow. Then, Chad's own brand of lightning dropped the doe!

COMING OF AGE

by NAHC Member Fred Colburn, Potterville, MI

When I turned 15 I was the happiest kid in central Michigan. It was a coming of age, because that was the first year I was old enough to go deer hunting with a gun.

I'm now in my 40s, but I can still remember that day like it was yesterday. It was a cool, sunny November 15. My brothers and brother-in-law came to the farm at 6:00 a.m. for a big breakfast before Dad, they and I went a mile and a half back to the woods of our 99-acre farm. Everybody knew where everyone else was so that we would not shoot in those directions, yet everybody would be within shouting distance if someone got a deer.

I chose to sit under an old walnut tree along the fenceline between the farm and the neighbor's property. But it was an uneventful morning and at about 10:15 a.m. Dad walked over to me to ask if I wanted to go back to the house for a short break. Being a typical kid and being frustrated at not seeing anything for three hours, I said, "Why not?"

As we were walking along the edge of some standing corn, we suddenly started hearing gunshots. My two brothers and brother-in-law shot about eight times between them. Dad said, "Here they come!" It was a doe and a buck. Then Dad and I shot; Dad was using slugs and I was using 00 buckshot. One of the deer went down about 75 yards from where we were standing. I asked, "Did I get it? Did I get it?" Dad laughed and said, "If it doesn't have a slug hole in it, I guess it's yours." Well, we got to the deer and it hadn't been hit by a slug, so it *was* my deer. I have hunted deer about every year since.

I have taken a course in conservation to learn more about the animals I respect. I believe hunting and sound conservation ethics are the surest ways to preserve game animals for all generations yet to come.

AMAZING
Animal Facts

 Dive right in. Ruffed grouse will dive head-first into a snowbank at high speed, then burrow several feet into the snow to create a winter burrow. The birds occasionally perish when the snowbank is ice-crusted.

Hold your head up. The horns of a bighorn ram may weigh more than 30 pounds.

The men's club. Ptarmigan divide into huge, gender-based flocks in the winter. Males retreat to alpine habitat, while the females stay at a lower, more sheltered altitude. When breeding season rolls around, each male breeds with only one female.

Planned parenthood. Although a wolf pack may number 25 animals, only one female—the *alpha* female—breeds. The leader of the pack, the *alpha* male, is the proud papa, although he sometimes allows the beta male to share in breeding.

 **Calling all hens!** During courtship rituals, male prairie chickens make a booming noise that can be heard from up to a mile.

Ready for the Olympics? Polar bears can swim as far as 50 miles without stopping, at a speed of up to 6 mph.

HUNTING PARTNER

*by NAHC Member David J. Page,
McFarland, WI*

It was still dark when I started the 60-mile drive, alone, to my brother-in-law's farm for the Wisconsin deer season opener. My wonderful wife would normally have been with me for our annual hunt, but this year was different. Every year was going to be different. What I didn't know was just how much my life was going to change for all future hunting seasons.

Just two and a half weeks earlier my first and only child was born—a son. Impatient as the rest of my family, he came nearly two months early. The excitement my wife and I felt was tempered only by the concern for the well-being of our son. He was born before I was completely ready to be a dad. Sure, I knew the day was coming, but I was supposed to have another two months to adjust to the idea. I was sure it couldn't be that hard; my own father survived three boys and four girls with the help of his own wonderful wife. My opinion, of course, is that they did a fantastic job.

Immediately after our son was born, he was whisked away to the infant intensive care unit. After checking that everything was okay with my wife, I went to ICU to see him. After being told by the nurses that my son weighed 5 pounds, 2 ounces, I commented that I'd caught bigger bass. The nurses apparently didn't appreciate my nervous attempt at humor. None of them even cracked a smile.

Our son couldn't leave the hospital when my wife did, so we went every day to visit and watch this little guy try to adjust to his new environment. I don't think that he knew what kind of life was in store for him, either.

I faced my first big decision as a dad. Could I enjoy opening day of deer season with my son still in the hospital and my wife visiting him without me? Without giving it much thought, I decided to stay home and, for the first time in more than 20 years, miss the short Wisconsin deer season. But my wife protested, explaining that I

needed to hunt this year, for my own sanity and also for the venison that we had grown so accustomed to having in the freezer.

I was there that November morning to watch the clouds roll across the horizon as the sun pressed against the cold, dark sky. A light dusting of snow made it a picture-perfect opening day. Tomorrow my wife and I were scheduled to bring our son home from the hospital, so today was my whole season. Luckily, I had drawn a hunter's choice permit that made it legal for me to take either a buck or doe. My strategy was to hunt for a buck until noon. If unsuccessful, I'd spend the afternoon just trying to fill my tag and ensure that my family would have some venison on the table this winter.

Thirty minutes after opening, a loud snort behind me interrupted my mental wanderings about life with my new son. I whirled around just in time to see a very large buck bounding off deeper into the thick woods. Shouldering the rifle, I had a fleeting opportunity and took what I thought was a well-aimed shot. I was wrong. Without even searching the snow-covered ground, I knew that I had missed. My dad, however, had taught me to respect the game I was hunting and the importance of following up every shot I took, even if I was sure I had missed. Dad had taught me a lot of those types of lessons. At that moment I couldn't help but wonder if I'd be such a good teacher for my son.

After I confirmed a clean miss, I struggled to concentrate on the stand and decided to take a short walk in the woods to warm up a little and reflect on the missed opportunity I'd have to confess to my wife. Moments later, as I crested an oak-covered ridge, I spotted a group of 8 or 10 does marching single file away from me. It wasn't yet noon, so I stuck to my plan and moved a little farther along the ridge. After I had gone a few yards, the crunching of brittle leaves caught my attention.

When a small doe appeared downhill from me, I froze in my tracks. I was very surprised when the noise I heard from her footsteps didn't stop when she did. The buck that was following her was not a record-book animal, but it was considerably larger than any other deer I'd taken in my life. One well-aimed shot ended my season and the doubts I had about being able to put venison in the freezer during my one-day season.

When I got home with the large 9-point buck, my wife was at the hospital visiting our son. She was there without me for the only time that our boy was in the hospital. I had that time to think about the next day, the day I would become an official dad.

My son's first hunting trip was on a warm October day in the cornfield where I hunt Canada geese. He was a very excited, healthy three-year-old. Nathan is nearly seven years old now, and we have hunted together many, many times. We enjoy our annual hunting camps where we live in the woods and hunt for squirrels, grouse and deer in the fall and turkeys in the spring. But shooting is only a small part of a much larger experience of being together to explore what nature has to offer and to live for the moments that burn into our memories as some of our greatest days ever.

We have had a number of them, but my son said it best when, on the last day of our most recent hunting camp, we were just an hour from packing up to leave. He looked me in the eye and said, "Dad, can't we stay just a couple more days?" He is my son and my hunting partner. 🖎

SUSQUEHANNOCK CLUB
by Joe Spaltro, Placitas, NM

The Susquehannock Club in Potter County, Pennsylvania, was established around 1938 by World War I veterans from American Legion Post #27 in Harrisburg. They purchased a log cabin on 100 acres with a stretch of trout stream. Membership has passed from the founders through their relatives, friends, friends of friends and some descendants. One of the founders, Col. Roy Taylor, was a key man in the formation of the Women's Army Corps (WACs) in WWII. As per the property deed and scuttlebutt, the cabin began life in the 1920s as a most isolated retreat for the alcoholic son of a Wellesboro physician.

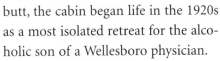

Every visit and meeting has been recorded in logs dating back to 1947. This wonderful history traces the club's evolution, with additions and losses. The entries vary from the severely laconic to humorous verbosity.

Notwithstanding all the deer, bears, turkeys, woodchucks, trout and shooting activities, the principal theme of the club has always been getaways of families and friends. It has been the place where many kids (including some of the now-senior members) have learned to enjoy and respect nature, trout hooks and firearms.

1. *b and c.* Cottontails tend to zig-zag and circle back when chased, so *a* is false.

2. *c.* Prime habitat usually holds one squirrel per acre.

3. *b and c.* Raccoons are good swimmers, so *a* is false.

4. *a.* Hares have 2 to 5 litters annually, so *b* is false. Both rabbits and hares run when pursued, so *c* is false.

5. False; fox squirrels as well as gray squirrels can have black pelts.

*"Another thing to remember, son: a buck is a buck until he's facing you—then, he's **Mister** Buck!"*

THE FUNDAMENTALS
SKILLS, EQUIPMENT AND ADVICE

Serious hunters know that basic skills and quality equipment are responsible for more game in the bag than all the luck in the world. Sure, a little luck doesn't hurt; but when you've got that royal elk sighted in the pins and your stiff jacket makes a noise as you draw, the only luck you're thinking about is bad luck. Spend some time reviewing the fundamentals. Get to know your equipment like the back of your hand, and practice with it until using it becomes second nature. Even if you're an experienced hunter, there's always something new to learn.

Buying A Deer Hunt

by NAHC Member Bob Humphrey, Pownal, ME

Outdoors shows are where outfitters book most of their deer hunts. You approach the booth, elbow your way through the crowd, and soon you're paging through albums containing photos of big bucks and grinning hunters. Before you know it, you're writing a check, and eight months later you're off on "the adventure of a lifetime." When you return, you dread that question from curious friends: "How did it go?"

"Well, it wasn't quite what I expected," is the best reply you can offer.

The outfitter didn't necessarily mislead you. You saw the pictures, asked a few questions, and soon imagined yourself tagging a trophy. But did you ask the right questions and really listen to the answers? Or did you only comprehend what made it through your optimism filter? Knowing what questions to ask and understanding the responses can take you a long way toward making your hunt enjoyable and memorable.

Success Rates

I recall booking a trip to Canada where the outfitter said, "Our bucks average around 120 Boone and Crockett Club points." This piece of information stuck in my brain. What I failed to consider was that even though some hunters were taking 140- and 150-inch bucks, many others were shooting substantially smaller deer. I also didn't ask the average success rate among hunters.

One of the statistics that outfitters use to sell a hunt is success rate—typically expressed as a percentage of the hunters who fill their tags. It sounds pretty straightforward, but it can be misleading. Believe it or not, a 15 percent success rate in Maine is exceptional. The average, even for residents who can hunt for 27 days, is around 10 percent. Furthermore, most outfitters hunt in the northern half of the state, where deer densities are much lower. If 15 percent of these guided hunters are taking bucks, they're doing very well.

Remember also that success rates at outfits catering primarily to bowhunters might rarely

be better than 50 percent. One fall, *North American Hunter's* Gregg Gutschow hunted with Life Member Shawn Woods, who runs Hawkeye Whitetails in Iowa. At the time Gregg arrived for his mid-November hunt, none of the previous hunters had taken a deer. All had seen bucks—many of which were Pope and Young Club contenders—and a number of hunters had missed their shots. Thus, some outfitters consider a reasonable shot opportunity a successful hunt. You can't ask for much more than one good chance on most fair-chase hunts.

On the other hand, success rates of 90 percent in a state like Alabama might not be all that outstanding considering that Alabama has a much longer season and a bag limit of a deer a day. During the 5-day hunt, 9 out of 10 hunters are tagging at least one deer, but how good are the bucks?

If you're after a trophy, success rates might not be the most important factor to consider. Trophy bucks are rare. And sometimes your best odds of taking a trophy are *not* in the same place that offers your best chance of filling a tag. If you're not after a trophy deer, remember that some outfitters have a minimum antler requirement at their operation. Sometimes you have to pay the outfitter a fine if you harvest a deer that doesn't have enough points or an inside spread that meets the minimum. Know what you're after and know any rules the outfitter has that differ from the regular state regulations.

"Guided" Hunts

Since most whitetail hunts are from treestands, "guided" means something different than it does to a Western outfitter who is attempting to get you within range of an elk or mule deer. Outfitters have different ways of defining what a guided trip is. Make sure you ask.

For many outfitters, "fully guided" means one guide per hunter. In contrast, on a hunt I took to Anacosti Island, my guided hunt consisted of one guide per four hunters. We were given a map and dropped off to hunt on our own, with instructions on when to be where if we wanted to be picked up and moved to another area.

In Saskatchewan, by comparison, nonresidents must hunt from a stand or be with a guide while hunting. Since a lot of the deer hunts there are stand hunts, your guide might simply be the person who drops you off and picks you up from your stand each day. Of course, there's nothing wrong with this, provided you understand it all before you pay for a hunt.

References

References are probably one of the best sources of information. Any reputable outfitter should be willing and able to provide you with a recent list of references. Unfortunately, most prospective hunters fail to use them—but *you* should. Also, the North American Hunting Club has an extensive file of Hunting Reports available to its members. For more information on the Club's "Approved Outfitters & Guides" booklet or for copies of Hunting Reports from fellow members, contact the NAHC Member Benefits Department at: P.O. Box 3401, Minnetonka, MN 55343.

"Yeah, I admit I don't cover much ground, but I figure if I sit here long enough something is sure to come by..."

How To Test Your Hunting Ammo

Rifle ammunition can be tested for accuracy, penetration and performance. An analysis of the results will reveal the best ammo for your hunting needs.

The most common test is for accuracy. It's not an exacting process, but necessary. To begin, gather the loads you wish to test. With one of them, check the rifle to be sure it's on paper. Clean the rifle. Shooting from a solid bench, fire five shots at the target. Regardless of where the bullets strike, be sure to hold the same sight picture for each shot. Do not adjust the sights during the string. You're shooting for a group, not sighting in the rifle.

Clean the rifle, put up a new target and repeat for each load. Allow the barrel to cool between strings and try to space shots evenly.

The ammo which prints the tightest group, regardless of where, is the most accurate in your gun. When your ammo selection is finally made, you'll adjust the sights to the proper point of impact.

Penetration testing is most commonly done with saturated newspapers or phone books. A couple of rounds of each brand are fired into a deep well of water-soaked paper from which the bullets are recovered. Then penetration is measured. Setting up a penetration range and maintaining consistent saturation is a hassle. And really all you'll discover is how far the bullet will travel through wet paper—not muscle, organ, sinew and bone. However, properly conducted, such tests can give you a *relative* comparison of penetration.

Performance testing is the most difficult, because what it comes down to is autopsying a lot of animals taken with the ammo to judge for yourself the performance in the field. Results are never conclusive. The best way to decide on performance is to rely on research done by the manufacturers.

Until you've set out exactly what you require of your hunting ammo and have researched several brands that *should* live up to those expectations, don't rely on accuracy tests as the final word. You may get sub-inch groups from a varmint load, but for deer hunting you'll be far better off with a proper big-game load that only groups in two or three inches.

—*Bill Miller*

RING THE DINNER BELL!

by various NAHC members

Deer camp is not just about hunting…it's also about fellowship, friends—and food!

"The name of my camp is 'Outpost 44' due to the fact that it is located so far from a public road and my CB name is 44. Inside the camp, in addition to the traditional deer mounts, I have hung rustic farm implements and old iron frying pans on the beams and posts made of cedar tree trunks. We always have a big breakfast for 15 to 20 hunters each Saturday and holidays during hunting season.

The standard breakfast consists of eggs, country sausage, venison smoked sausage, Southern grits, orange juice, coffee and hot biscuits. Breakfast is really a social event. Lunch for most hunt days consists of venison and some type of beans."
–*William V. Griffin, Pollocksville, NC*

"Deer camp started in my house as a place to meet, see how everyone was doing and show off the deer. The first few years would include serving a mid-morning breakfast to our real close friends. As the group grew, I began serving some food after the hunt since most people showed up without eating. Then it got to the point that not all the people could get in the house and with Wisconsin's snow and rain, it was making a real mess in my house. I then built a new garage to become deer camp with a walk-in cooler, meat cutting room, stereo, TV, VCR, electronic dart board and a bulletin board for pictures of hunters and their deer. An official name was also given to camp: 'Lyle's Big Bucks Deer Camp.' Now during the nine-day season I have food and refreshments every day including an opening-night buffet." –*Lyle Lenz, Ripon, WI*

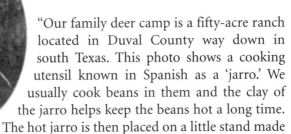

"Our family deer camp is a fifty-acre ranch located in Duval County way down in south Texas. This photo shows a cooking utensil known in Spanish as a 'jarro.' We usually cook beans in them and the clay of the jarro helps keep the beans hot a long time. The hot jarro is then placed on a little stand made of deer antlers to protect the table from the heat."
–Marcus C. Canales, Rio Grande City, TX

"Dad and I built 'the cabin' in the fall of 1956. Every stick came from our property in the best deer country of upstate New York. I was thirteen then. Dad passed away eight years later, but the traditions have been preserved now for well over forty years. The list of venison recipes could go on forever, but the top few will always be venison stew; liver, bacon and onions; spiedies; silver dollar steaks; and pickled hearts. Venison jerky, of course, has always been the snack food of choice." –Fred Hungerford, Oneonta, NY

"My wife Jamie and I bought our deer camp in January of '98. We have a Coachman that sleeps six or seven people on a 50 x 100-foot deeded lot. It is used all year round, but is my primary archery hunting spot. I consider our camp to be the best investment our family has made to date. For anyone thinking of buying a camp: I hope you and your family can enjoy yours as much as us. Bye for now; we will put a mountain pie on the campfire for you."
–Stan Marchlewski, Creighton, PA

Stan Marchlewski
& daughter Crystal

SHOTGUN FIT

by *Bob Allen,* North American Hunter *columnist*

Once I asked one of America's top trapshooters, "What's the biggest thing that sets apart the best shooters?"

Without hesitation, he answered, "Somewhere along the line, each of them found a gun that fits properly and then had the sense to stick with it."

In shooting clinics, the first thing I check is the shotgun's fit to the shooter. I'm always amazed to find out how many hunters don't know about gun fit.

The four components to gun fit are: length of pull, pitch, height of the stock and width of comb. (All but the last are shown in the illustration on the facing page.)

1. Length of pull is the distance between the trigger and the rear of the stock or recoil pad. Most guns come from the factory with a pull length of 14½ inches to 15 inches, which might be too long for a young person or a woman and not long enough for a big man.

2. Pitch is the angle at which the gun stock is cut off prior to attaching the recoil pad. Pitch is measured between the line of bore and the cutoff. Most guns come from the factory with about 1½ inches down pitch, which is okay for most shooters. Pitch determines how a gun "kicks" to a certain extent. A stock with zero pitch will recoil straight back, but could slip off the shoulder as the gun is swung. Reverse pitch would make the gun slide off your shoulder in a downward direction on recoil or when gun is swung. Too much down pitch will make the gun buck against your face.

3. Height of the stock or "drop" in relation to the top of the barrel or rib offsets the point of impact of the shot pattern. When the gun is placed against your shoulder and your face (cheekbone) is firmly placed on the comb of the stock, you should be looking right down the barrel. If the barrel seems to be tipped up, the stock is probably too high, and the gun will shoot high. If it is so low your eye can't see the barrel, you'll probably shoot under everything.

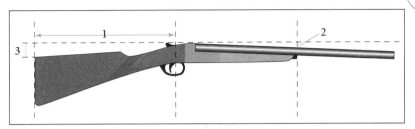

1. *Length of pull*
2. *Pitch*
3. *Height of stock or "drop"*

4. Thickness of comb affects how well your shooting eye lines up with the barrel. A comb too "fat" for you will cause your eye to be off to one side of the line of bore. By the same token, a comb too thin may cause your eye to be off the line of bore on the opposite side.

To understand the basic principles of shotgun fit, one must understand the philosophy of shotgun shooting. A shotgun has no rear sight—only a front sight. Your eye constitutes the rear sight, and to be effective, the pupil of the eye must line up with the line of bore both laterally and vertically. The comb width affects lateral fit, and comb height affects the vertical alignment.

To illustrate how sensitive this is, consider a rifle. A rifle has a stationary front sight and a movable rear sight. Moving the rear sight one "click" up will move the bullet impact up by one inch at a hundred yards. One click sideways will move bullet impact one inch sideways at 100 yards, and so on. Compared to a shotgun, the fit of the stock on the rifle means little because your eye is forced into position to properly line up the sights. The sights give you an immediate visual indicator that your eye is out of line.

To determine if your shotgun has a proper length of pull, put the gun to your shoulder and place your cheek on the stock. I'm an advocate of a stock as short as possible without your thumb hitting you in the nose. Your cheek should rest comfortably forward on the stock. Shoot a stock as short as you can without getting bumped in the nose, but not so short that it will pull away from your shoulder when you swing the gun.

Your build has something to do with the proper pitch as well. A man with a big belly and a body that slopes sharply down from the shoulder might need more down pitch in order to seat the gun comfortably. I use different pitches for different types of shooting. For trap singles, I have a zero pitch. The gun comes up easy, kicks straight back, and because I use it only for singles, I don't care if it kicks down from my face after recoil. In contrast, when I shoot doubles, I use 1¼-inch down pitch to assure that the gun won't kick away from my face. I use the same for hunting.

To assess width and height of comb, face a mirror, close both eyes, mount your gun and aim at the mirror. When you have it where you think it is correct, open your eyes and look down the barrel in the mirror to the pupil of your eye. If the barrel line of the bore isn't lined up laterally after several such tests, then possibly your comb is too thick or too thin. This same test will also check comb height.

If your comb needs adjustment, there are several ways to correct it. An adjustable one can be installed for about $200.00 and many gunsmiths offer this service. Meadow Industries makes a "Convert-a-stock" pad, offered in several thicknesses, that fastens to the stock with Velcro. There are lace-on leather pads.

I guarantee that having proper gun fit will make a dramatic difference in all your shooting! ☞

Tungsten Shotshell Comparisons

	TUNGSTEN-IRON	TUNGSTEN-POLYMER
Recommended Usage	Pass shooting	Shooting over decoys
Typical Target	Large ducks; geese	All ducks; upland game
Pattern Coverage	90% patterns	80–85% patterns
Pellet Energy at Target	Greater than lead	Equal to lead
Barrel Requirements	Steel-approved barrel OK	All barrels OK

Courtesy of Federal Cartridge Company

SUCCESS

Roy Bowers

Hometown:	Sugar Grove, WV
Species:	Grizzly Bear
Weapon:	.338 Winchester Mag, 225 gr.
Hunting state:	Tatshenshini River, British Columbia (Canada)
Guide:	Northwest Big Game Outfitters, guide Rick Hilderson

"The hunt was challenging because of the mountainous country. Awesome bear, great guide. Hunt of a lifetime."

An Arrow Dynamic

by Chuck Adams, North American Hunter *columnist*

Most bowhunters are constantly concerned about the business end of their arrows—broadheads that fly true and perform efficiently on game. And when trouble occurs, they fail to see the real culprit at the other end. You see, like any fighter jet needs a good pilot, even the best broadheads need proper fletching to steer the arrow like a missile to the target. It can make or break arrow flight.

So let's back up to the back of the arrow and make certain we've got both ends right.

Birds Of A Different Feather

The age-old debate regarding feathers and plastic vanes rages on. Which is better for the average bowhunter? In my mind, the choice is cut and dried. With compound bows, it is almost always possible to achieve complete fletching clearance with plastic vanes. By tuning a gener-

---

Rx For The Right Starter Bow

Here are a few factors to consider in selecting the proper compound bow.

■ **Axle-to-Axle Length:** A bow with a 43- to 46-inch axle-to-axle length is best for novice or intermediate shooters. These medium-length bows yield a smoother release and better accuracy than shorter bows. ■ **Draw Weight.** For most adult men, a compound with a 50- to 65-pound or 55- to 70-pound draw weight will be best. This is a manageable draw weight and is capable of cleanly harvesting deer-sized game. ■ **Draw Length** varies from shooter to shooter. Visit your local archery pro shop for help in accurately measuring your draw length (at left). ■ **Let-Off.** A compound with a 60 to 65 percent let-off is the most comfortable. It can be kept at full draw with a minimum of strength, to allow for proper aiming. ■ **Wheels.** Moderate-speed or energy wheels are best for starter bows. Typically, these are smoother, more accurate and more forgiving.

---

ously center-shot modern bow, experimenting with arrow rest styles and rotating nocks until there are no scuffs on fletching or rest when talcum powder is applied between shots, you can achieve excellent accuracy.

Plastic vanes are durable, waterproof, and quiet in an arrow quiver. When correct fletching size and angle are used, flight stability is easy to achieve.

Feather fletching, by comparison, is fragile, quickly weather-wilted and noisy in a quiver. However, feathers are essential with old compound bows, recurves and longbows because such designs do not have more modern center-shot handle risers. Fletching almost always impacts the bow handle during a shot, and unlike plastic fletching, feathers flatten on impact to prevent wobbling flight. Similarly, feathers are the sure cure for clearance problems with some hunting arrow rests that chronically cause difficulty with full-size hunting fletches.

If you suffer prolonged problems with broadhead accuracy despite careful tuning, feather fletching is also best.

Feathers create 50 percent more drag on the rear of an arrow than vanes of the same size.

If you opt to shoot feathers, treat fletching with silicone powder or spray to retard wilting in wet weather. Steam matted feathers over a teapot to restore them to original shape. Replace frayed feathers immediately to avoid excess noise in flight or poor accuracy.

Even top-quality plastic vanes sometimes become misshapen. Heat these with a hair dryer, stove or direct rays of the sun, and they'll usually bounce back.

Steering Sizes

Fletches for hunting arrows must be larger than those on target shafts. This is necessary to stabilize a broadhead.

For arrows weighing less than 475 grains, three 4-inch fletches or four 3-inch fletches provide good accuracy. The main advantage of four-fletch is that you cannot misnock the arrow. No matter how it snaps on the string, bow-to-fletching geometry remains the same. By comparison, three-fletch requires you to nock the arrow with a cock vane (off-color fletch) pointing away from the bow, straight up or straight down.

Tailspin

Target shooters often shoot straight-fletch because non-spiraling vanes or feathers allow better clearance with most arrow rest designs.

But hunters need spiraled fletching to stabilize broadhead flight. Spiraled fletching rifles the arrow through the air like a bullet, canceling a broadhead's tendency to dart or dive. Spiraled fletching also increases rear-end arrow drag, which enhances accuracy.

Numerous tests by archery companies have proven that one degree of fletching angle is best on hunting arrows. Such fletching configuration causes the arrow to rotate one full turn during every 30 to 36 inches of forward travel.

Used with three 4-inch vanes or four 4-inch vanes, an average 500-grain deer arrow with 1-degree plastic fletching slows down about 1 foot per second (fps) in every 10 feet of forward travel. So on a 30-yard shot, the arrow slows down

about 9 fps. This slow-down rate normally produces superb flight with broadheads from a well-tuned bow.

Broken Wings

Plastic vanes are commonly damaged during target practice by impact from other arrows. To remedy small rips and holes near the fletching edge that cause excess drag and noise in flight, simply snip out these defects with scissors. The small V-shaped cuts left behind will not affect accuracy.

More severe damage to feathers or vanes requires new fletching. Most archery dealers re-fletch shafts for a modest fee, or you can do it yourself. I prefer the convenience, satisfaction and cost-effectiveness of fletching my own arrows. I can quickly "roll my own" arrows to precise specifications for less than ready-made arrows cost. I can also replace damaged vanes or feathers.

If you're serious about bowhunting, consider do-it-yourself fletching. You'll be steering yourself and your arrows toward optimum accuracy. ✒

PLAN FOR SUCCESS

by Gregg Gutschow,
NAHC staff member

No matter if you're getting ready for the annual firearms deer season in your home state or planning your first Western elk hunt, a lot of effort goes into preparation. Part of that planning should include how you are going to care for the cape and skull of a big game trophy you'd like to have mounted.

"Preparing a game head trophy requires a lot more than just removing the skin from the animal," warns Marv Gaston, NAHC Member and owner of Taxidermy Unlimited in Burnsville, Minnesota. "Having the knowledge of what to do is an absolute must."

Gaston says approximately 20 percent of the capes cus-tomers bring him each year have been ruined by improper field care. His first piece of advice is to visit your taxidermist *before* your hunt—no matter if it's a deer hunt on the Back 40 or a Colorado elk hunt. Most taxidermists, he assures, will be willing to give 15 minutes or so of instruction that will help the average hunter prepare and preserve a cape until it's delivered to the taxidermist.

Here are several points your taxidermist will likely cover with you about trophy care:

✓ **Keep blood off the cape.** Deer, caribou and sheep hair is hollow and absorbs blood. Skin the game in such a manner that the cape remains as blood-free as possible. Stream-rinse blood out of the cape as soon as possible. Though taxidermists can bleach out blood-stained capes, this weakens hair and the life of the mount. Mountain goats and bears have solid hair; thus, blood stains are not as critical.

✓ **Determine what kind of mount you want:** head and

shoulder, life-size, etc. Learn how much cape is needed, and remember—too much is better than not enough.

✔ **Skinning and fleshing.** Here's where a little personal instruction from a pro will really pay off. Your taxidermist will probably have a diagram showing how to make the cuts up the back of the neck and around horns or antlers. He can also show you techniques to remove skin cleanly around the eyes and mouth. If you bag a buck close to home, take the trophy to the taxidermist before the butcher. Most taxidermists prefer to do the caping themselves, and it's best to do this as soon after the animal is field dressed as possible.

✔ **Ears, lips and nose.** If you're on a remote, do-it-yourself type of hunt, you'll have to be able to turn the ears and lips and split the nose. Basically, splitting these parts of the cape allows this tissue to dry out faster to prevent spoilage.

✔ **Salting the hide.** Again, if you're away at deer camp for an extended period or in remote wilderness, you'll need salt, unless you have access to a freezer. Five pounds of salt at base camp is adequate for each deer-sized shoulder mount—rub salt into all parts, then fold it up skin to skin. For full-body skins, you'll need 10 to 15 pounds of salt. Don't use rock salt; it doesn't absorb moisture sufficiently. Use table, canning or feed salt.

Gaston says many hunters make the mistake of trusting that outfitters and guides will take the time and effort to ensure that the cape and head from your big-game trophy will be properly prepared for delivery to a taxidermist. Ask first! Find out if the hunt fee includes this service. Inquire whether or not a local taxidermist is available to handle this sort of prep work.

According to Gaston, capes from large deer and elk and other big-game species are in such high demand because so many are ruined each fall. Plan for success and you'll come home with excellent meat and a beautiful trophy. ☞

Caping An Elk

This sequence, from the NAHC book *Elk Essentials* by Bob Robb, shows how to remove the basic cape, and head, so a taxidermist (or you) can complete the detailed caping work.

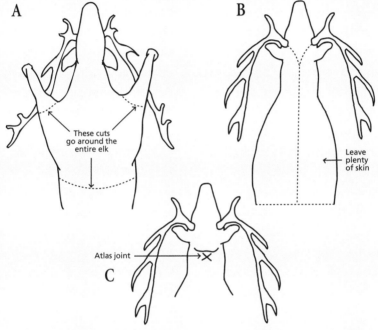

A. With the elk on its back, make the cuts shown, going completely around the elk's body.

B. With the elk on its chest, make the cuts shown and then completely remove the skin.

C. Use your knife to carefully remove the head at the Atlas joint (where the head meets the neck). Do not saw through the joint, but rather work your knife in the joint until you can free the head.

Airborne Antlers: Check Before You Go

When you're making arrangements for a remote hunt, ask the outfitter if the skulls of large animals are brought out whole. Many bush pilots cut the skull in two to get the rack in the small plane, ruining your record rack.

CARRY A CAMERA

by Tom Carpenter,
NAHC Staff Member

We all have pictures of deer hanging from a meatpole or laying on a garage floor, or of pheasants or ducks or some other gamebird unceremoniously arranged on a tailgate, sidewalk or patch of backyard grass. While these pictures make *good* mementos, there's a way you can make *great* mementos. It's easy.

Just carry a small, lightweight, portable pocket camera with you as you hunt. Even the disposable 35mm cameras available today do a great job.

Store the camera in your game vest, a coat pocket (inner ones work great) or your pack. The weight is negligible—but imagine: having pictures of you and your deer in the field, right where it fell, before you've field dressed it; holding up a duck to the rising or setting sun; posing with an antelope as the prairie and blue sky sprawl behind you; or admiring a grouse in the tag alders where you got it.

Remember to arrange the animal in a natural position, wipe off blood, stuff any lolling tongues back in. Try shooting the picture with the sun off to one side or the other and use a

"Looks like the bucks stop here..."

flash to fill in the shadows that will be created. If it's a "people" or "people-and-game" shot, don't shoot directly into the sun or with the sun at your back; the subjects will be under- or over-exposed. Slightly overcast days are perfect for pictures—the light is even and from all sides. On really cloudy days, be sure to use the flash. Always take more than one shot, to make sure at least one turns out.

Of course, if you have a camera along, there will also be plenty of chances to take photos of the countryside and of your hunting companions. In time you'll be surprised—you'll come to treasure these types of shots as much as your "success" shots.

Packing a camera is easy and little to no trouble these days. Expensive, heavy gear is great, but a light and portable outfit will go where you go and let you hunt hard—but be there for those special moments when you need it most.

Maybe your photos won't be masterpieces, but they'll be good enough to help you recall the day and what happened, and the excitement of it all. And that's what pictures are all about anyway. ❧

IMPROVE YOUR STALKING SKILLS

by NAHC Member Tex Hill,
Hereford, AZ

A leather-clad hunter moves as silently as a shadow. Upwind, the deer sees no movement, hears no sound, scents no danger. The hunter is patient. He moves only when the deer's attention is elsewhere. At last, within range of his home-made bow, arrows and broad-heads, he strikes! His family will not go hungry tonight.

There was a time when stalk-ing game was as ordinary a skill as driving a car is today. It wasn't something unusual—it was man-datory. Many modern hunters have forgotten how to stalk. The enormous range of modern hunting tools has made very close approaches less necessary. Paved highways isolate us from the land through which we pass, reducing our sensitivity to subtle mes-sages our ancestors read as easily as we read the road map. The environment where most of us live and work is flooded with so much noise and movement that our dulled senses block them from our conscious observation.

All of us like to believe we are at home in the woods. Too many times, though, we crash through brush like a cattle stampede ... not because we don't know better but because to earn a living we have to spend more time out of the woods than in them.

In order to improve our stalking skills, we must under-stand what they are. Everyone knows about soft footfalls. Most avoid smoking, coughing, talking and stumbling, but there is more to successful stalking than that.

We all realize the impor-tance of not being seen by game. But it is not enough to outfit yourself with any old fatigues. You must choose a camouflage pattern which will be most effec-tive in the terrain and weather conditions where you hunt.

Know what type of cover you will most commonly encounter in your hunting range and choose colors and designs that blend into the landscape. Grease paint colors for face and hands are also important for the same reason. Remember that skin is highly visible even when you're stationary.

When required to wear blaze orange, consider the broken-field types if they are legal where you hunt. Avoid carrying items that rattle, jingle or hamper freedom of movement. You should carry keys, for example, in a soft leather pouch inside a pocket. Anything that makes noise, cannot be properly secured, or is too bulky is better left behind.

Study the ground over which you will move. Must you cross large open areas? Are there dead leaves, dry grass or thick brush? Water crossings? All these can be silently traversed, but techniques differ for each type of obstacle.

Learn to separate the impossible from the possible. Even a stealthy mountain man of yesteryear couldn't silently walk over a carpet of dry leaves. Instead, he went around. When there are no alternate routes, there are ways to cross such obstacles, but none of them are easy. Patience is the key.

You can use wind, rain, snow and even bright sunlight to your favor. The best stalker is one who can make the most of the conditions on any day afield.

Use rain or snow to cover your approach. A soft rain is your greatest ally when dry leaves and weeds litter the ground. Nothing muffles footsteps better than wet vegetation.

Breezes can be unpredictable, and a knowledgeable stalker is always alert. There will be times your scent is suddenly carried to the quarry without warning. It's part of the game. However, understanding wind currents can often prevent this.

Never step without knowing what lies underfoot, but don't keep your eyes on the ground all the time. Glance down, memorize details and hazards, plan each step, then proceed cautiously over that distance. Never try to move too far or too fast. Walk five or six steps, then check and double-check your path.

Learn to spot areas of concealment. Plan your approach to take advantage of trees, brush, rocks and land contours. Have an alternate route in mind if anything should suddenly increase the risk of being seen or heard.

When you spot game, remain motionless. Study it. Try to anticipate in which direction the animal will move. Figure out the best way to intercept it or close in on it from your position. Move only when you are reasonably sure a successful stalk is possible. It is far better to pass up one animal when the odds are against you than to risk spooking other animals.

Do you smell yourself? Such things as aftershave, deodorant and clothing laundered with scented detergent are foreign to the wilderness. If you're camping, seal your hunting clothes in plastic to avoid contaminating them with odors.

Since an animal's sense of smell is far more acute than a human's, you must be extra alert to odors that will identify you or disclose your position. Being careful is not enough. Hunt into the wind; end of discussion.

Contrary to what poets say, the wilderness is not a place of silence. Water splashes; wind blows; branches sway and crack; birds flutter; animals grunt, snort and dislodge pebbles.

Human noises are not part of the wilderness. We make unnatural noises like coughs, metallic sounds, labored breathing and heavy footsteps. At times, though, human noises can be used in your favor. For example, someone once started a chainsaw, and the sound allowed me to swiftly cross a gully filled with loose gravel. The deer heard people cutting firewood almost daily, so they ignored the racket.

My wife and I often use bird calls to communicate with each other because deer ignore such ordinary sounds. Voices, even whispering, would warn every animal in the area that humans were approaching. Of course, you must imitate only local birds and avoid distress or alarm calls.

If you should happen to crunch a twig or roll a pebble, freeze. Your quarry will hear it, but may not be alarmed since harmless things could also cause that noise. Take one more step, however, and they will recognize it as approaching danger.

Game animals can instantly identify certain sound patterns as threatening. Herbivores wander slowly and aimlessly, while predators move steadily and purposefully. Dry grass brushing against cloth does not sound at all like the same grass swishing against hair. Remember, when you cannot avoid noise, imitate natural sounds and sound patterns as closely as possible.

A short stride is best for walking. Feel the ground with your toes before placing any weight on that foot. If you feel sticks, leaves or loose rocks, try another spot. Learn to walk toe to heel; you'll be much more able to sense what is going on underfoot before committing yourself to that step.

If conditions warrant it, don't feel foolish about lying down and crawling on your belly. So what if you get dirty or look silly? You just might collect that once-in-a-lifetime trophy!

Footwear depends on the ground conditions, weather and personal comfort. My choice has always been a style of moccasin we in the Southwest call Apache boots. Their soft leather soles allow you to feel things before you put weight down. The tops reach to the knees and either lace or roll up for a snug fit that protects your legs from thorns, brambles and other hazards. They should fit snugly, but without discomfort.

If you wear hiking or combat boots, examine them for good fit, high tops and quiet flexibility. Don't try to save a few dollars on boots; buy the best you can afford. Snow boots offer necessary protection in winter, but choose them carefully. Most are made from synthetic materials rather than leather, and may be noisy.

Even with a high-powered rifle, moving soundlessly is just as important as when hunters went afield with homemade bows. If you want to increase the odds of making every hunting season successful, learn the basics of stalking. Practice often, under all kinds of conditions, until moving silently has once again become an instinctive ability. ☞

The Born Loser

— R STUBLER —

• THE FUNDAMENTALS •
Ammo, guns and other important matters

1. *True or false:* A stainless-steel bore brush is better than a bronze brush, which can cause the bore to rust.

2. Tungsten-iron pellets in shotshells are:
   a. 20% heavier than lead, so they fly farther when shot but with looser patterns.
   b. 94% as dense as lead, and they deliver more pellet energy on-target than lead.
   c. The same weight as lead, but they pattern more tightly.
   d. 73% as dense as lead, making them faster to the target.

3. How does bullet construction affect performance? (mark all that apply)
   a. Thin-jacketed bullets shatter on impact, especially at higher velocity, so are good for varmint hunting.
   b. Thin-jacketed bullets allow the bullet to penetrate more deeply before expanding, making them good choices for heavy-skinned game.
   c. The rear lead core in a partitioned bullet provides deeper penetration, while the front half is designed to mushroom.
   d. A boat-tail bullet is more subject to wind drift than a straight-tail, so is not a good choice for long-range shots.

4. When you increase the choke on a shotgun (from cylinder to modified, for example), what happens?
   a. The pattern spread becomes wider, but the shot arrives in a tighter string.
   b. The pattern spread stays the same, but the pellets arrive on-target with more energy.
   c. The pattern spread stays the same, but the shot arrives in a tighter string.
   d. The pattern spread becomes narrower; on-target energy does not change.

5. What does the name of the .30-30 rifle signify?

  a. The rifle has a bore diameter of .30 inch, and it was first introduced in 1930.

  b. The diameter to the outside of the rifling grooves is .30 inch, and the recommended bullet weight is 130 grains.

  c. The rifle has a bore diameter of .30 inch, and the original bullet was propelled by a 30-grain smokeless powder charge.

6. If there are slits through the fabric of the patch after you've shot your muzzleloader, it could mean: (mark all that apply)

  a. You used too much powder.

  b. The ball-and-patch combination is too tight for the bore.

  c. This is normal; if there are no slits the patch is too small.

  d. Rust in the barrel may be shredding the patch.

7. Mark all statements about scopes that are true:

  a. A smaller exit pupil is better than a larger one, since the image will be more focused.

  b. A larger objective lens enhances target image by allowing more light to enter.

  c. Parallax occurs when the image of the target is not properly focused on the viewing plane.

8. How do oval speed cams on a compound bow affect arrow flight?

  a. Flatter trajectory

  b. Faster flight

  c. Higher accuracy

9. *True or false:* To shoot sabot slugs, you need a barrel without a screw-in choke because these interfere with sabot slugs.

10. When you're shooting a rifle downhill, adjust your aim by:

  a. Aiming lower than for a level shot

  b. Aiming higher than for a level shot

  c. No adjustment necessary

Answers are on page 192.

"Out Of Sight" In Wyoming

by NAHC Member Bruce
Bohnenstingl, Minneapolis, MN

It was the opening day of Wyoming's antelope season, and I was anxious to do some hunting. We had just arrived from Minnesota after a long drive; we hadn't even checked into the motel in town yet, but had headed straight for the ranch where we would be hunting. There were a few hours before dark, and we wanted to make the most of it, so we set off on foot.

I should preface this story by saying that I'd spent many, many hours—and many cartridges—sighting-in at the long-distance range back home. So when a nice buck suddenly appeared on the other side of a hill I had crept up, I felt sure that the 200-yard shot was within my reach. I eased off the safety and pulled the trigger. Imagine my surprise when the bullet skidded harmlessly in the dirt a foot behind the antelope! The animal took off, unscathed, after looking quizzically in my direction. Obviously, my scope had been jarred during the drive over the bumpy ranch roads.

The other members of my hunting party came up to see what had happened with the shot and commiserated with me about my rotten luck. The nearest range was a long ways away, but I didn't see any option; I'd have to take the time to go there.

Then one of the guys offered a suggestion. I should tell you a little about Lance first. He is a really nice guy and would give you the shirt off his back. He also is a sucker for gadgets, especially anything having to do with his main passion—hunting. If it was new and foolish, Lance would pop for it. His hunting trailer was filled with all sorts of what-is-it gimcracks, and he thought he had just the ticket for me now.

"The ticket" turned out to be a neat portable target holder. Made of heavy metal, it folded up cleverly into a compact bundle. So while Lance and most of the others continued their hunt, I set up the holder at the base of a small cliff and prepared to re-sight my scope.

I paced off one hundred yards, as near as I could make it, and took aim at the bull's eye.

Clang! I nailed the right side of the horizontal arm that held the target. The arm didn't break through, but it sure had a good nick out of it, about 6 inches to the right of center. I wondered how much Lance had paid for this thing and also how one was supposed to avoid doing the very thing I had just done. Oh well, it could have been worse; at least the con-traption was still standing. I had originally sighted in to be dead-on at 300 yards, so the height was

Nick in right arm

Centerpost (still standing!)

about right at 100 yards. I aimed to the left of the bull's eye and shot.

Ca-chunk! This time, my shot snapped off the left side of the horizontal arm completely, barely missing the vertical center-post. I re-adjusted the clips on the maimed right arm so it would still hold the target, and tried one more shot. I aimed low and to the left, since my two pre-vious shots had been uniformly high and to the right.

I guess bad things happen in threes, because my third shot was dead-on center and hit the vertical centerpost, snapping it neatly in two. The only thing left standing was the bottom of the centerpost, which was still firmly in the ground.

I really don't consider the event a waste, because I was able

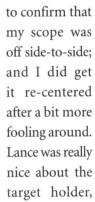

to confirm that my scope was off side-to-side; and I did get it re-centered after a bit more fooling around. Lance was really nice about the target holder, too, when I handed it back to him in pieces, since the device was new and could be replaced when we got back home.

By the way, I did get a nice buck two days later. And I've learned my lesson: no more shooting at game after a long, bumpy ride without re-checking my scope. After all, why let a lit-tle thing like an out-of-align-ment scope ruin a hunt ... and maybe a friendship?

Field Judging Trophies

When you're hunting, you often need to make snap decisions about the quality of the animal in your sights. Here are some quick tips you can use. Every time you see a game animal—even a mount at a store or friend's house—train yourself to assess its trophy potential using these tips, until it becomes easy.

Whitetail Deer

■ A buck's ear is 6 to 8 inches long; use 7 inches as an average. A Pope and Young buck must have at least two 6-inch-long points on each antler; compare ear length to tine length to judge this, as well as the length of the main beam.

■ The tips of a mature whitetail's ears are usually 16 to 18 inches apart when the deer is alert. Use this information to judge inside spread.

■ Learn to count the number of "tines up" to quickly judge numbers of points. Concentrate only on the tines on one side, and only those pointing up; you'll add in the brow tine and main point later. In the illustration at left, the buck shows 3 "tines up" so this is a 10-point buck.

■ To judge mass, compare the size of the eye, which is about 4 inches around, to the thickness of the antler beam. A main beam that is as big around as the eye, or bigger, is likely to be a good buck.

■ A mature buck generally has a thicker neck with a blocky head, while a young buck has a sleeker, more streamlined head and neck. The old buck will probably have a rough coat, compared to the smooth coat of a younger buck.

Antelope

■ The typical antelope ear is about 6 inches long and makes a great measuring "tool" for the length of the cutter (prong) and horns. If the horn is twice as long as the ear, for example, the antelope has 12- to 13-inch horns—not exactly a trophy. But if there is some "hook" left in the horns at that point, you could have a good 14 or 15 incher on your hands. Thick horns are a bonus in scoring antelope racks, so be sure to consider that factor as well.

Mule Deer

■ The ear of an adult mule deer is almost a foot long, and the spread from eartip to eartip (which is 16 to 18 inches in a whitetail, as shown on the facing page) is about 24 inches. If you see a muley whose spread is two inches or more beyond the ear spread, you may be looking at a trophy.

■ The antler of a trophy mule deer will show mass all the way to the antler tip, rather than turning spindly at the ends.

Bears

■ A live bear in the wild looks big, almost no matter what. To get a more accurate reading of the bear's size, look at its ears. Large-appearing ears indicate a small bear, as do ears that seem to stand out on top of the bear's head. If the ears appear to come out of the side of the bear's head and seem to be in proportion with the rest of the body, you've got a good-sized bear.

Dall Sheep, Stone Sheep

¾ curl →

Full curl

■ Draw an imaginary line from the base of the horn through the nostril, and another perpendicular to that from the back of the eye (dotted lines at right). In a full-curl ram, the tip of the horn will touch the line that runs from the base to the nostril; on a ¾ curl, the horn will touch the line that runs through the eye.

Hunter's Recipe File

Rose's Awesome Barbecued Rabbit

- ½ cup all-purpose flour
-     Garlic powder and pepper, to taste
- 1 rabbit, cleaned and cut into pieces
-     Vegetable oil as needed
- 1 8-ounce can tomato sauce
- ⅓ cup brown sugar
- 1 tablespoon liquid smoke
- 1 teaspoon minced onion
- ¾ teaspoon chili powder
- ⅛ teaspoon garlic powder
- ⅛ teaspoon dried parsley flakes

Dash crumbled, dried summer savory leaves

Heat oven to 350°F. Combine flour with garlic powder and pepper; dredge rabbit pieces in flour mixture. In large skillet, brown rabbit pieces in vegetable oil over medium-high heat. Transfer browned rabbit pieces to baking dish. Combine remaining ingredients and pour over rabbit. Bake for about 1 hour, or until tender.

from NAHC member Michael G. Roylance, Laramie, WY

FIELD CARE: FACTS AND MYTHS

by NAHC Member Lon Lauber, Wasilla, AK

Family, friends and house guests dining at the Lauber homestead frequently rave about the delicious wild game portion of the meals. I'd like to claim four-star chef status or the uncanny ability to select tastier game on the hoof. However, neither is true.

What makes our game meat so delicious starts in the field. Call me old-fashioned, but I find great satisfaction in playing the role of hunter/gatherer—especially when the end result is tasty and healthy. With the help of an expert meat processor, I'll share a proven system for improving the quality of game meat.

"In order to make the best meals from your wild game, one needs to start with an animal well cared for in the field," says Doug Drum, proprietor of Indian Valley Meats near Anchorage, Alaska. Drum, who grew up around a slaughterhouse in Michigan, has lived in Alaska nearly 30 years. His business handles and processes between 275,000 and 300,000 pounds of meat per year.

"There are theories on game meat care in the field," Drum says. "I use a proven method based on principles employed in the commercial meat processing industry. The aim of this technique is to make life harder for bacteria and flies by creating a cool, high-acid environment; this slows bacteria growth and limits their food sources by bleaching out blood. It also makes a protective glaze coating, thus controlling flies."

Use The Right Game Bag

Drum advises never using plastic game bags, as they hold in heat and don't permit air circulation. He recommends using high-quality game bags, those made from a breathable, bug-resistant material. They must be strong enough to carry the meat yet allow maximum air circulation, and the mesh must be tight enough to keep flies out. My personal game bag favorites are from McCoy Enterprises. Real McCoy game bags are made of a durable cotton blend. This stretchable, interlocking knit provides a one-size-fits-all format, and the bags are washable and reusable. Jagged bones frequently ruin other game bags; however, the knit design of Real McCoy bags prevents cuts and holes from "running." I've been using McCoy bags for three years now. Even after lugging massive moose muscle, they work like new.

Another trick I learned from Drum is to treat game bags with a citric acid blend. "While flies might land on a bag treated with a citric acid solution, they won't hang around long; the citric acid stings their feet," he explains. "Additionally, the citric acid helps inhibit bacteria growth."

Citric acid works because bacteria grows rapidly at a pH level of 7.0, while the pH of a lemon is about 2.35. The citric acid solution on the bag dramatically drops the pH level, helping to kill bacteria and repel bugs. To make a citric acid solution, combine the juice of three lemons, one large bottle of lemon juice concentrate and one small bottle of Tabasco sauce. Soak the game bag

in this solution for 20 minutes to one hour, then allow it to air dry completely (not in your dryer!). Store in a large zip-top bag.

The acid pH level of game meat fluctuates according to the animal's activity level, Drum explained. "For example, a spooked animal that has been running hard will have a low blood sugar level, which causes the lactic acid in the muscles to be higher and the pH level to go up," he explains. "This, in turn, gives the meat a darker color and stronger flavor. That's why, in terms of top-notch table fare, a clean kill is so important."

Cooling The Meat

The sooner your game meat is cooled, the better tasting it will be. It's important to bleed, gut and skin the animal as soon as possible. This allows body heat to dissipate more rapidly, thus lowering the carcass temperature. If you're hunting near a stream or lake, it's safe and recommended to dunk the meat in cool water, thus cooling the meat even faster. However, Drum cautions not to cool the meat completely in water, but instead to allow the meat to retain just enough heat so it will dry by itself once it's out of the water.

Most of my game care experience comes from cold-weather hunting, so I asked NAHC Bowhunting Advisory Council member Bob Robb what he learned from his years in California. There, he harvested a mule deer in the early coastal season every year for 15 years. "That season opens August 10 and can see daytime temperatures soar past 100°F," Robb remarks. "Many friends believed getting meat wet would destroy it, but I found just the opposite to be true. Many times I shot a buck in the morning several miles from camp. By the time I got it back, the temperature was almost 100°F. The secret was to bone it out, then submerge the meat in a small stream until it cooled down. I'd lay a space blanket in the water first, weighing it down with rocks, then lay the meat on it to keep it clean. Not only did the stream cool the meat, it leached out excess blood too. Once the meat was cooled, I loaded it in game bags and packed it back to camp. By then it was usually dry, so I immediately put the meat on ice. The result was excellent venison for my family's table."

Storing Meat In The Field

Once the carcass temperature has been lowered, it's important to dry the meat. The key is to hang the meat out of direct sunlight where any breeze will gently blow across the carcass. Excess moisture can be rubbed off the meat with your hands, or wiped away with paper or cloth towels.

"Once excess moisture has been removed, apply the same lemon juice mixture mentioned above in a light coat over the entire carcass," Drum advises. "This will create a high acid protective glaze over the meat while it is drying. Once the meat is dry, it can be placed in game bags and re-hung." According to Drum's exhaustive studies, hanging game meat for five days at about 42 degrees provides the best combination of flavor and tenderness. Hanging wild game longer will further tenderize the meat, but will result in flavor loss. On remote hunts, Drum recommends quartering the carcass immediately and de-boning meat just prior to departure.

Old Man Winter

"When an animal is killed in below-freezing temperatures, it's important to leave the skin on, or skin while the animal is still warm and cover the carcass with a tarp or sheet of plastic (a space blanket works too) for 20 minutes to one hour," Drum instructs. "If the meat's surface starts to freeze, cover the plastic-covered carcass with snow to insulate it so freezing does not occur until rigor mortis sets in."

Rigor mortis is the process where the muscle tissue starts to stiffen up. This might take several hours, depending upon the size of the animal and ambient temperature. If the carcass freezes before rigor mortis sets in, the pH level will not drop to around 5.3. Then your meat will be tough, chewy and flavorless.

Home Cutting Tips

With so many hunters butchering at home, knowing how to cut the meat is important to ensure proper flavor and texture.

"For tender steaks, cut the meat *across* the grain," Drum recommends. "The grain gives the meat its tough texture, so by cutting across it you're helping break it down. When you cut *with* the grain, you get meat with jerky texture."

I've learned to cut, package and freeze meat as small roasts. Then I partially thaw the roasts (to make slicing easier) and cut the steaks to the thickness everyone prefers. Also, a roast has less surface area than steaks, helping to minimize freezer burn.

Drum also says that freezing meat at temperatures between minus 5 and minus 10 degrees increases its shelf life. Moreover, if you've thawed too much meat and wish to refreeze it, you can. First dry it out, then re-wrap it. You should use this meat within 60 to 90 days, he warns.

Proper game meat care and scrumptious, healthy table fare are my pride and joy. Being prepared with the right tools for the job and learning how to care for meat properly will reward you. Family, friends and houseguests will rave for more. That means you'll just have to keep hunting hard to put more meat on the table!

Jim Baichtal

Hometown:	Thorne Bay, AK
Species:	Sitka Black-Tailed Deer
Weapon:	Custom .54 cal. Hawken Rifle, 90 grains of FFg, Patched Round Ball
Hunting state:	Alaska

"The hunt was seven years in planning. Weather and terrain had thwarted several attempts. In 1998, my partner and I boated 50 miles and climbed 10 hours up from the shore to the alpine where we made camp. The next morning we climbed higher, spotting the buck in his bed. The stalk got me within 30 yards, but the buck exploded from his bed, forcing me to make a 60-yard running shot. The massive buck scores 121⅝ Boone and Crockett points, making it the largest Sitka blacktail ever taken with a muzzleloader."

HOW HUNTING RIFLE AMMO WORKS

Though it happens in less time than it takes to blink an eye, knowing what goes on in a cartridge during firing is important to understanding ammo. The intense pressures that cartridge and rifle undergo are mind-boggling when you really think about it.

The cartridge fits relatively loosely in the chamber of a rifle when the bolt is closed. Upon the release of the sear when you squeeze the trigger, the firing pin comes forward and strikes the primer.

This causes a small explosion that sends a flame through the flash hole in the base of the case. The flame ignites the carefully measured charge of smokeless powder.

The powder burns rapidly and violently in the tight confines of the case. The burning creates gas and pressure so intense that it enlarges the brass case to the full dimension of the chamber and sets the cartridge back tightly against the face of the bolt.

When the pressure becomes so great, the bullet is forced out of the neck of the case into the barrel.

In the barrel, the cartridge engages the rifling. It's another tight squeeze as the gas pressure drives the bullet down the barrel. The lands and grooves of the rifling violently spin the bullet. This spin imparts accuracy to the bullet as it heads to the target.

Great gas pressure forces the bullet to the muzzle, then rushes past as the bullet exits, bound for the target.

During the first part of the flight, a properly sighted rifle causes the bullet to arc above the line of sight, but as gravity and wind resistance take over, it drops back toward earth to penetrate the target where it was aimed.   *—Bill Miller*

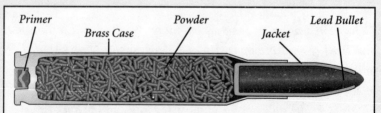

Primer   *Powder*   *Lead Bullet*
Brass Case   *Jacket*

To create an accurate, efficient hunting cartridge, all components must be precisely matched. Selecting the right combination is the hunter's challenge. Being able to rely on the research and development of ammunition manufacturers in creating a wide range of loads is the greatest advantage to buying factory ammunition.

HOW SHOTSHELLS WORK

One common misconception about shotgun shells is that the length listed on the outside of the box is the unfired length of the shotshell hull. But the standard lengths (2¾-, 3- and 3½-inch) are of the cases with the crimps open.

A look down a shotgun barrel from the back end quickly reveals that it is not perfectly cylindrical or smoothly tapered from front to rear. At the very rear of the barrel is the chamber, where the shell is located when the gun is loaded.

When you pull the trigger, the firing pin comes forward, striking the battery cup primer in the base of the shell. Just as in a rifle, an explosion results, sending a spark forward to ignite the carefully measured charge of smokeless powder.

The powder burns rapidly and violently in the small area of the case behind the wad. The increase in pressure inside the case is so sudden that it in effect outgrows the space available, thus pushing the wad and shot charge forward. Before the forward movement is great enough to relieve the pressure, the gas expansion slightly buckles the base of the wad. One of the wad's important functions, this buckling prevents this initial violent jarring from deforming the rearward pellets.

When the top crimp is forced open, its leading edge is to the rear of a section of the barrel known as the forcing cone. The wad, with its payload of pellets, enters the forcing cone and is constricted to standard barrel diameter.

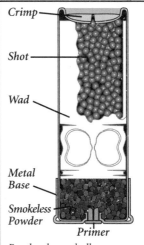

Powder charge, hull construction, and the amount, type and size of shot are variables the hunter chooses when buying factory ammo.

Depending on the degree, if any, to which the barrel is choked, the wad and shot charge are further constricted as they approach the muzzle. During this entire journey down the tube, the shotcup portion of the wad protects the outside pellets from deformation that would occur as they scrub past the barrel wall.

Wind resistance begins to peel back the petals of the shotcup as soon as it exits the barrel, slowing it dramatically. It falls to earth a short distance down range, leaving the shot charge to spread into its pattern and travel unimpeded to the target. —*Bill Miller*

"…Just get me 911…I don't have an address…"

HUNTING CAMP ALMANAC

Hunter's Recipe File

Danny's No-Peek Venison Stew

Using a deep Corningware dish, layer the following in the order given:

1½–2 pounds venison stew meat, cut into stew-sized pieces

- 1 medium onion, sliced
- 2–3 carrots, peeled and sliced
- 1 turnip, peeled, quartered and sliced
- 2 potatoes, peeled and sliced
- 1 10¾-ounce can condensed cream of celery *or* cream of mushroom soup
- ½ envelope onion soup mix

Cover and cook at 275°F for 4 hours; *do not peek.* Serve hot with fresh, hearty bread.

from NAHC member Martin C. Carver, Surrey, BC

NAHC Life Member
SUCCESS

Nathan Gilbertson

Hometown:	Breckenridge, MN
Species:	Pronghorn
Weapon:	.257 Weatherby Mag., 120 gr. Nosler SB Handloads
Hunting state:	Montana

"This buck had 15½" horns, scoring 79⅝ before mounting. Somehow I got within 40 yards of this fellow ... he never knew I was there. Just enough wind, just enough terrain."

LEAVE ROOM FOR A GPS UNIT

from NAHC's Elk Essentials
by Bob Robb

The Global Positioning System, or GPS, is a highly accurate navigational system developed by the United States Department of Defense that can be used anywhere in the world. It's based on a group of 21 working satellites, plus 3 in-orbit "spares." Precise orbits of each satellite assure that at least 4 are in view at all times

from any position on earth. Because of the satellites and the sophisticated receivers that we use in conjunction with them, GPS units can be used 24 hours a day, in virtually all weather conditions.

GPS works by measuring the time it takes a radio signal to reach the receiver from a satellite, converting that time into distance and then determining exactly how far it is from the transmitting satellite. By measuring the distance from 3 of the 4 satellites always in view, a position can be fixed in latitude and longitude. It's a "Star Trek" version of the ancient art of triangulation— fixing a position using landmarks that include everything from rocks and trees to the stars themselves. And by reading the 4th satellite—the one most directly overhead—the GPS unit also provides your current altitude.

One of the advantages of this navigation system is that you can use it to get from point A to point B time after time, even in the dark. This can be done during scouting trips or the actual hunt itself. You can also save waypoints and coordinates and pass them along to a buddy, who can go to the exact spot you did by plugging the coordinates into his own GPS unit. ✐

Good ... And Good For You!

According to the U.S. Department of Agriculture, here's how a 3-ounce cooked portion of various game meats compares with other meats in the nutrition department.

Meat	Calories	Fat (grams)	Cholesterol (milligrams)	Protein (grams)
Elk, leg cut	135	1	67	24
Venison, leg cut	139	5	62	22
Pheasant	126	4	41	20
Quail	140	6	47	21
Rabbit	119	7	57	15
Beef round steak	189	8	81	27
Beef tenderloin	174	8	72	24
Beef brisket	223	13	77	24
Ground beef (72% lean)	248	18	77	20
Ground beef (82% lean)	213	12	84	25
Lamb leg roast	153	6	74	24
Lamb loin chop	183	8	80	25
Veal cutlet	155	4	112	28
Pork shoulder	207	13	82	22
Pork loin, top	219	13	80	24
Chicken breast, with skin	167	7	72	25
Chicken breast, skinless	140	3	72	24
Turkey, dark meat	159	6	72	24
Turkey, white meat	133	3	59	26
Bass, broiled	167	3	62	18
Salmon, broiled	140	5	60	21
Halibut, steamed	111	3	62	20

MAKE A LIST, CHECK IT TWICE

The lists on these pages are from *Elk Essentials* by Bob Robb, and *Secrets of the Turkey Pros* by Glenn Sapir (both published by the North American Hunting Club). Make a copy of this list, and mark each checkbox as you pack the item.

Backpacking Checklist

- ☐ Backpack and rain cover
- ☐ Daypack or fanny pack
- ☐ Spare pack pins
- ☐ Tent with rainfly
- ☐ Sleeping bag and sleeping pad
- ☐ Space blanket
- ☐ Stove, filled fuel bottle
- ☐ Cooking pot (coffee pot)
- ☐ Lexan spoon, fork
- ☐ Quart-sized water bottles (2)
- ☐ Food (1½ to 2 pounds per person per day)
- ☐ Waterproof matches or butane lighter
- ☐ Nylon parachute cord (50 feet)
- ☐ Toilet paper
- ☐ Small hand towel

- ☐ Liquid camp soap
- ☐ Hunting knife, whetstone
- ☐ Compact bone saw
- ☐ Headlamp and flashlight, new batteries
- ☐ Fluorescent flagging (½ roll)
- ☐ First aid kit, Band-Aids
- ☐ Ibuprofen, personal medication
- ☐ 1-inch cloth athletic tape
- ☐ Moleskin
- ☐ Spare eyeglasses
- ☐ Game bags (4)
- ☐ Water purification tablets
- ☐ Compass, topographic maps
- ☐ GPS unit
- ☐ Heavy-duty trash bags (2)
- ☐ Hunting license, necessary tag

For your daypack, carry the following items from the list above:

- ☐ Space blanket
- ☐ 1 water bottle
- ☐ Lunch/snacks
- ☐ Matches or lighter
- ☐ Parachute cord
- ☐ Toilet paper
- ☐ Change of socks
- ☐ Hunting knife, whetstone

- ☐ Flashlight or head-lamp, batteries
- ☐ Fluor. flagging
- ☐ Band-Aids
- ☐ Medications
- ☐ Cloth athletic tape
- ☐ Moleskin
- ☐ Spare eyeglasses
- ☐ Compass and maps

- ☐ GPS unit
- ☐ License and tag

During late season, add:

- ☐ Warm gloves
- ☐ Stocking cap
- ☐ Light vest/jacket
- ☐ Packable Gore-Tex rain suit

Turkey Vest Checklist

- [ ] Small flashlight
- [ ] Folding saw or pruning shears
- [ ] Knife
- [ ] Leatherman-type tool
- [ ] Compass
- [ ] Cough drops
- [ ] Insect repellant
- [ ] Compact binoculars
- [ ] Decoy(s) and stakes
- [ ] Mouth diaphragm calls
- [ ] Box call
- [ ] One-handed box call
- [ ] Slate, aluminum or glass call
- [ ] Striker(s) for the above-listed calls
- [ ] Call maintenance kit (sandpaper, chalk, small plastic bag)
- [ ] Locator calls
- [ ] Soft-pouched drinks
- [ ] Energy bars
- [ ] Toilet paper in a resealable plastic bag
- [ ] Raingear
- [ ] Shotgun shells
- [ ] Pen
- [ ] String or wire ties
- [ ] Surveyor tape to mark locations
- [ ] Pocket-size camera
- [ ] First aid kit
- [ ] Face mask
- [ ] Gloves
- [ ] Seat cushion
- [ ] Waterproof matches and/or cigarette lighter
- [ ] Space blanket
- [ ] GPS unit

Muzzloader's Checklist

- [ ] Rifle
- [ ] Percussion caps
- [ ] Capper
- [ ] Blackpowder or Pyrodex
- [ ] Powder measure
- [ ] Powder flask
- [ ] Bullets
- [ ] Short bullet starter
- [ ] Synthetic ramrod
- [ ] Nipple/breech plug wrench
- [ ] Pre-lubed patches
- [ ] Bullet lube
- [ ] Speed loaders
- [ ] Small balloons (for barrel protection)
- [ ] Cleaning supplies (powder solvent, clean patches, ramrod attachments, light gun oil)

1. False; most gunsmiths recommend against stainless-steel bore brushes because they are too hard and can damage the bore.

2. *b.* 94% as dense as lead, with more on-target energy than lead.

3. *a and c.*

4. *d.* The pattern narrows with a tighter choke.

5. *c.* The rifle has a bore diameter of .30 inch, and the original bullet was propelled by a 30-grain smokeless powder charge.

6. *b and d* are possibilities if there are slits in the used patch.

7. *b and c.* The larger the exit pupil, the easier it is to keep the eye aligned with the sight picture, so *a* is false.

8. *a.* Oval speed cams provide flatter trajectory.

9. False; special rifled chokes are available to help stabilize sabot slugs.

10. *a.* The slant-range effect, which occurs when you are shooting downhill or uphill, means that you must lower the point of aim.

JOHNSTON FARM FOR HUNTING DOGS

"Man, I'm getting tired of this—when do we get to go into a field?!"